Reflections of Life

This book is donated by the Landfall Writers Group
to the New Hanover County Library.
We hope you enjoy our stories.

Reflections of Life

Copyright © 2017 The Landfall Writers' Group

All rights reserved. No part of this book may be reproduced, stored, transmitted or copied in any form, electronic or mechanical, including photocopying, recording or transmitting by any information and retrieval system, except by written permission of the contributing authors.

You may contact any of the authors at the following email address: LandfallWriters@gmail.com

Published by Landfall Writers' Group
Printed by Blurb
Edited by Dalene Bickel

Printed in the United States

Disclaimer: Each story contained in this book is based on the contributing author's recollection of events, related to the best of his or her knowledge. No errors, oversights or harm were intended for any individual, organization or company.

We would like to dedicate this collection of stories to our families, readers and friends.

We hope, after reading Reflections of Life, *that you are encouraged to write and tell your stories.*

About the Cover Art

"I have tried to represent the Landfall Writers' Group—our diversity and our intimacy. I saw tall buildings reflecting themselves into one another and I have tried to duplicate that. It isn't about the reflections, but about us, as a cohesive group."

— Diane Torgersen

CONTENTS

Charlotte Hackman
Roll Back
A Near-Death Experience
My Bucket List

Ed Hearn
My Fiftieth High School Reunion
A Special Encounter
Why Am I Still Here?
A Day at Cascade Plunge
A Funny Moment
Memories of My Dad
Becoming "The Hunted" While in Africa
A Memorable Movie
A Bucket List Moment
My Most Unforgettable Individual in Sports
Achieving My Long-Term Athletic Goal
Aging Together
An Evening of Star Gazing and Reflection

Dick Nasca
Going to the Woods
Dormy
Missing on Call
My Victory Garden
Night on the Town
Passing the Tube
Shepherd's Pie
Sidewalk Roller Derby

Neighborhood Memories
Slippery Slope
The White Line

Marie Varley Gillis
It's All about the Brownies
Business Casual

Sarah Hardman Giachino
Battle of St Lo France-Operation Cobra
I'm the One You've Been Looking For

Diane Torgersen
Cheating and Redemption
My Medical Career
Creative Awareness
Critiques
Home Is Where Different Is

Doris Chew
A Conversation about Death and Dying
Lessons from Number 2 Daughter
Ocean's Edge

John Roper
A Medical Miracle
Holy Mary, Mother of God

Myrna Brown
Ferris Wheel
In the Disquiet of My Mind

"I am a writer of books in retrospect. I talk in order to understand; I teach in order to learn"
— **Robert Frost**

FOREWORD

This collection of stories was written by a group of writers of all levels who joined together in 2015 to form the Landfall Writers' Group (LWG), named after the members' residential community in Wilmington, North Carolina.

LWG serves as a collaborative forum to share ideas, offer constructive feedback, and promote the writings of its members.

The reader of this book will experience a variety of stories, including memoirs, family history, fiction and nonfiction. This is the second book written by the LWG. *Pieces of Life* (published in 2016) was the first anthology of the group's creative efforts; however, its members have collectively published eight books and numerous magazine articles.

We all have unique stories to tell, and we encourage you to share yours...while you can still remember them!

CHARLOTTE HACKMAN is an author, playwright, public speaker and actress living in Wilmington since 1993. *The Strength to Let Go,* her first nonfiction book, was published in 2015 under the pen name Jo Henry. Her play, *Change of Life* was produced off-Broadway in New York. Major movies, television series and stage credits are included in her acting resume.

Charlotte received a BS in Education from University of Central Missouri with a major in English and speech minor. She taught high school for several years in Texas and New York.

She holds a Master's Degree in psychology from Texas A&M University. While living in Texas, she worked in family and individual counseling.

She and her husband, Ed, grew up in Jefferson City, Missouri, where they went to high school together. They moved to Texas after college and while pursuing their careers, took time to start a community theater in Bay City, Texas. After moving to Wilmington, Charlotte served as president of the board of Big Dawg Productions for several years.

They have one son and he and his family also live in Wilmington. Charlotte loves making up stories with her granddaughter Peyton and sometimes turns those into plays or puppet shows.

Charlotte enjoys playing poker, reading, playing golf and traveling. You will still see her occasionally on a local stage. Much of her writing is done in the summers in the North Carolina mountains.

ROLL BACK
Charlotte Hackman

My husband Ed got a temporary job assignment in Montreal, Canada in the winter of 1976. We arrived on New Year's Eve and moved into our downtown high-rise apartment and celebrated with a six pack of Molson beer and Guy Lombardo on TV.

We had taken a few ski vacations and decided our stay in Canada would be the opportunity to get serious about the sport. On the weekends, we took day trips to the surrounding ski areas where we were honing our skills on the icy slopes.

In early March, we decided to take a "big" weekend trip to Mont Treblant and spend two nights there. The forecast was for several inches of snow and we had never skied on "powder," the term used for inches of new snow.

It was here, early in our skiing days, we encountered a "roll back" on a chair lift, something that is never supposed to happen. It's also when I realized a big difference between Boy Scouts and Girl Scouts! Ed was an Eagle Scout and I had been an avid Girl Scout.

If you have snow skied, you know what a chair lift is. If you haven't, the chair lift is that thing that looks like a porch swing that carries you up the mountain, suspended from cables held on tall, tall poles. You wait in line, slide over to the chair on your skis, stick out your butt, sit, and ride up the mountain.

A chair lift will stop from time to time as you are riding up the mountain because somebody fell getting off up at the top. The first few times we skied, falling as we got off the lift was my standard procedure. Though Ed always warned me to Be Prepared (the Boy Scout motto), I was never quite *prepared* to disembark. We made a great sight as we approached the top with me frantically asking *"NOW? Should I lean forward NOW? What do I do with my poles?"* and Ed yelling, "Don't grab me! Be prepared to get off!"

Anyway, that's why the chair lift stops sometimes so the guy running the lift can untangle the husband and wife and the skis and the poles that have fallen in a heap at the top of the lift. But never does a chair lift start moving down the mountain backwards. *Never*!

That morning in Canada we had a foot of new snow (powder). We had made one run down the mountain and got on the chair lift to go up again. The chair stopped—not unusual. We looked down, enjoying the view of the colorful skiers on the newly fallen fluffy snow.

Just then, a very strange thing happened. The chair started going backward very slowly and then stopped.

I looked at Ed asked, "Was that strange?"

"Yes." Ed is a man of action and few words.

About that time, we started going backwards again—and picking up a little speed. Then we could feel the cables jerk like something was trying to stop us, and we stopped with the chair gently swinging.

"I don't think this is supposed to happen, do you?" I asked.

"No." answered Ed.

We did this *roll back–stop–roll–stop* routine a couple of

more times and the skiers on the ground were now all stopped, looking up at the chair lift. Some of them shouting, "Jump!" which seemed out of the question since we were three stories in the air. I was definitely not prepared for this wild and unexpected event.

Like a good Girl Scout, I started thinking about those other people who had been behind us further down the mountain. What had happened when they got back to the "get on place" going too fast to get off? Would the chairs fly off that big turn wheel at the bottom?

We began moving backward again, really fast, and people were again screaming, "Jump!" Easy for them to say.

I looked at Ed and asked, "Are you gonna jump?"

He was bent over and I thought maybe he was sick or something. "Are you OK? Are you gonna jump?"

"I dunno," said Ed the Eagle Scout as we felt some more jerks and slowed down to an almost stop.

"Well, once we go over that ridge, it's really a huge drop off and we can't jump then. I bet people that jumped near the bottom are all piled up," I said with visions of bloody bodies.

Ed the Eagle Scout bent over again. *Is he gonna throw up or what?* I wondered.

About that time, *shooosh,* we took off backwards like a racehorse out of the gate and gained speed. I have no real explanation for what happened next.

I looked at Ed and said, "We're not going get any closer to the ground. I think I'm gonna jump!" And I did. *With my skis on!*

Somehow that foot of new snow looked soft and fluffy—until I hit it. Trust me, I cleared that powder in an instant. I was not *prepared* for the pain. It knocked all the wind out of me, too. With my first gasp of air, fearing the worst, I called out to Ed (which rhymes with dead). Was he now one of those bloody bodies I had envisioned at the bottom of the lift?

"EEEEDDDDD!"

In a quiet voice like an angel from above I heard, "I'm here."

My God, he's dead and already an angel. His voice is right above me.

I turn my injured body, spitting snow to look up and see him swinging above me on the chair lift, *without his skis*. The chair lift had stopped the instant I jumped.

I watched in amazement as a gentleman climb up one of the ski lift's support poles (which our chair just happened to stop beside), pull our chair over and help Ed down. Ed was able to climb down the pole whereas others had to wait up in those chairs for hours to be taken down.

My injuries were relatively minor: bruised ribs and a few pulled things here and there. By some miracle, I hadn't broken a leg —jumping with my skies on.

Once Ed knew I wasn't seriously injured, he started.

"Sweetheart, for God's sake, if you were gonna jump, why didn't you take off your skis? In that kind of wild and unexpected situation, you need to think fast and Be Prepared. It's a miracle that you didn't break a leg."

How do I explain that as a good Girl Scout, whose promise includes "to help other people at all times, especially those at home," I had been concerned about those other people and especially worried about him. And then I realized why he had bent over.

"You were taking off your skies? That whole time I was

worried about you being sick and puking on the people below us, you were taking off your damn skis?"

On that unforgettable trip to the mountain, I learned a very important lesson: To be concerned is nice, but to be prepared is better.

A NEAR-DEATH EXPERIENCE
Charlotte Hackman

After the terrifying experience of the chair lift roll back on a ski slope in Canada, one might suspect that I would have given up the sport. I did not. Forty years later, I was still an avid skier…well, as avid as one can be with only a week or two a year spent on the mountain.

It's safe to say I was more proficient and I no longer fell getting off the lift. I could manage to ski a black diamond difficult trail…assuming it was groomed and *not* full of moguls. I was a "careful" skier and didn't take a lot of chances or let my speed get out of control. I had very few falls. Perhaps I was ultra careful not to fall because getting up was very difficult for me.

We were on our annual trip to Lake Tahoe when our son lectured me about not wearing a helmet on the slopes.

"Mom, it's just crazy to be out there without a helmet," he implored.

"But I don't fall, and I don't get out of control," I responded. Besides, I liked my cute little ski hat that matched my jacket.

"Here, you have to wear this." He thrust a ski helmet at me and insisted I put it on. He had convinced his dad to start wearing one the year before, but I was the hold out.

I started to protest again, but finally, I reluctantly gave in. It wasn't nearly as cute as my ski hat.

As I skied that first day ever in a helmet, I found it wasn't as uncomfortable as I had feared. In fact, it wasn't uncomfortable at all and it kept my head and ears nice and warm.

The second day as we headed to the lifts, I didn't argue about the head gear. I just put it on, much to our son's delight. The older half went one direction and the younger set another.

We got to Diamond Peak overlooking Lake Tahoe early that morning and the slopes were still icy. We went up the chair lift to the top and started down. Skiing on icy terrain is a bit tricky and a little unusual for the Tahoe area at that time of year, but we all managed to navigate the hard ice and headed up for a second run.

Part way down the mountain, there is a spectacular view of the lake and a spot where we all liked to stop to catch up with the group before tackling the second half of the run.

I was traversing the narrow trail to our gathering place and waving to my cousin when I caught an edge of my ski. Before I knew what was happening, I had fallen over the edge of the gentle trail onto the steepest part of the downhill slope…a place I never attempted to ski.

I was on my back, sliding headfirst down the steep, icy slope. I wanted to swing my legs around, but then I pictured myself flying head over heels down the mountain. Yet I knew I needed to turn to get my skis pointed downhill to try to stop myself…but that wasn't happening…and I was picking up speed. Everything started to feel like it was happening in slow motion and I remember every detail like it was just yesterday.

Suddenly, I realized the terrain was sloped toward the trees. I remember thinking, *Oh God, not the trees!* just before I collided into the first massive evergreen.

And with that, I started slamming from tree to tree, with my skis still on, and my hands over my face, with the poles still attached. *When is this going to stop?* I wondered.

I continued my pinball-like bouncing, with my head smashing into trees and limbs until finally, I came to a stop, straddling a tree and believe it or not, my skis were still on.

I caught my breath and took stock to determine that yes, I was still alive and amazingly, nothing seemed broken.

My cousin had witnessed the slide and subsequent jaunt through the trees and was on the edge of the slope further down where it wasn't so steep, yelling frantically.

"Are you alright? Talk to me." He was starting to take his skis off to help me get out of my awkward position.

"I'm okay. I think I can get out." I released a ski, climbed out of the tree and started to climb to where he was anxiously waiting. I was so thankful that I had finally stopped what had felt like an extended trip through the woods. And in fact, it had been a long distance from where I had tumbled over the edge.

The rest of the group started to arrive at "the scene," with questions of "What happened?" "Are you hurt?" And from my husband who was late to get there, "What are you doing down there?"

I was a bit shaken, but happy to be alive. I checked my bindings, put my skis back on and proceeded to get down to the bottom of the mountain without further mishap.

We all decided to take a short lift ride to a little coffee and snack cabin with a heavenly view of Lake Tahoe. Once there, I decided I was done for the day as a variety of limbs and body parts were starting to hurt. After a brief snack, I urged the rest of the group to go on and I would just wait there and enjoy the view until their next rest stop.

I assured my husband I was fine, as he was reluctant to leave. He said he would be back to check with me soon. I took the helmet off and placed it on the outdoor table where I was sitting. I got a little bored so decided to get out my cell phone and call my two best friends.

First, I called Joyce in Pennsylvania.

"Hi, it's Charlotte calling you from the mountains."

"Oh, how are things going?"

"Well, I think I just had a near-death experience," I said. I tend to be a bit overdramatic at times and she knows that, but when I explained my accident on the mountain, she was... sympathetic?

"You're out of your mind. You shouldn't be skiing at your age anyway." *Well, sort of sympathetic.*

That was followed by not exactly what you expect to hear from a best friend. "I really don't have time to fit a funeral into my schedule right now, so I'm glad you survived," she said good heartedly.

With that, I said a brief good-bye and hung up the phone. I repositioned myself on the metal bench (my entire body was beginning to get uncomfortable) and then called Barbara in Wilmington.

Seeking a little more compassion this time, I once again explained the scary experience in detail, ending with how I was straddling a tree...with my skis on.

She was full of concern and I was getting the strokes I was

seeking until she delivered her ominous message: "You know, this isn't over yet."

"What? Of course it is. I survived with no broken bones, but maybe some bruises."

"Oh, you could still die," she said with absolute certainty. "You could get a blood clot and that could be it."

With that, I said a hasty good-bye and hung up. I was not going to call any other friends at that point!

I stood up to go get a cup of hot chocolate and found nothing in my body wanted to move. However, I managed to shuffle in to get the drink and as I returned to my table, a young man from the ski patrol spotted my helmet. Then he noticed my disjointed movement as I tried to sit down.

"Are you okay?" he asked.

"I think so." I replied. "I just took a tumble down the mountain and I got a little stiff sitting out here."

"Holy cow, is this your helmet?" he asked, as he picked it up and turned it around in his hands. None of us had really looked at the helmet until that moment. It had four deep gashes and was scraped and scratched all over. *Wow!*

"Are you sure you're all right? That had to be a hell of a fall to do this!" he exclaimed.

"It was, indeed," was all I could say.

He checked me out a bit and got a couple of ice bags to move around what was going to become some very nasty bruises. *He* was very sympathetic.

"You know this helmet is destroyed, right? You can put it in the trash, but lady, it probably just saved your life."

That was a sobering thought! Maybe I needed a glass of wine.

About that time, the entire group slid in for lunch. My husband decided it was time for me to try to go home and put my feet up. There was just one little issue…I had to *ski* down to the bottom because there was no other way to get there. My cousin suggested the ski patrol could take me down in one of the baskets for injured skiers.

"No way. That scares me to death to think about it. I would probably die of a heart attack the way they ski so fast with that thing," I protested. In all honesty, it probably also has something to do with me always needing to be in control, so I opted to try to ski down.

There was groaning and moaning and a couple of curse words, and that was just to get my skis back on. Skiing down to the bottom was agony, but I managed.

In the next few days my body turned several shades of blue and purple, followed by green and yellow. It was a bit painful, but I felt so blessed for so many reasons.

On that unforgettable trip to the mountain, I was reminded of two valuable lessons. First, sometimes you can learn very important things from your children, if you will just listen to them. Our son, with his knowing insistence about helmets on the ski slope, had probably saved my life. Second, be careful about the sympathy you're seeking from your best friends. It still makes me laugh to remember those phone calls.

I knew I would return to the mountains once again. And I did.

MY BUCKET LIST
Charlotte Hackman

Many years after my terrible experience on the ski lift in Canada and after my near-death experience in Tahoe, I still loved skiing.

In January of 2017, I went to Sugar Mountain in North Carolina to check two items off my bucket list. First, I wanted to ski for the first time with my six-year-old granddaughter and secondly, to finally be old enough to ski for free, as I was coincidentally going to celebrate my birthday on this trip.

Peyton, our granddaughter, was excited about giving snowboarding a try. Our son was an accomplished boarder and Michelle, his wife, had taken up the sport also. My husband Ed, being the wise old Boy Scout, had given up skiing a few years earlier…about the time of my near-death experience. We settled into our rental house in downtown Banner Elk and hoped the forecast was correct, which was calling for cold temperatures with a chance of snow.

We played games, went out to eat and waited for the temperature to drop…which it did. We gathered around the fireplace, the first move in soaking in the mountain winter ambiance. However, the fireplace wouldn't work. The pilot light would come on, but when we tried to light the fire, it would go out. Perhaps that was an omen.

We went out to eat for my birthday dinner and it was lovely. The downside was that I ate way too much and then, of course, had to have dessert…it was, after all, *my birthday!* I had a rather miserable night with an overstuffed tummy, but eagerly looked forward to the next day.

I was finally old enough to get that free lift ticket and I wasn't going to miss the opportunity. I guess they assume if you are still able to ski at my age—or are crazy enough to try—they will reward you with not having to pay to put your body through the rigors of the sport.

I had purchased a new puffy ski jacket just for this trip. The first thing I noticed was having put on three layers of clothing made it more difficult to bend over to put on ski boots. I couldn't decide if my difficulty breathing was due to the altitude or the gigantic meal from the night before. *Maybe it was the puffy jacket?*

I arrived at the bottom of the lift breathless with excitement…or just breathless. I looked a bit like the Michelin Man in that puffy jacket and helmet.

Peyton was waiting anxiously for her Mimi to head up the mountain with her Mom and Dad on a six- person lift. We got off the lift at the top of the mountain without any problem. Our son Colin, gave Peyton a few more instructions and off she went. She was a natural. She managed to control her speed and could change directions and would just sit down to make any corrections or rest. Michelle was snowboarding cautiously behind Peyton while Colin was usually just in front helping Peyton if needed. I was usually a little behind the group just soaking in the sight.

We took a break at the bottom of that first run and got some hot chocolate and a cookie for Peyton. The thought crossed my mind I had accomplished my goal, so perhaps I should be a senior ski bunny for the rest of the day and watch from the giant windows of the bar. We noticed the hill was getting more crowded compared to earlier that morning, too. But Peyton changed those thoughts with her pleas of "Come on Mimi, let's go again!"

Peyton was getting more skilled with each run, while I had sort of peaked out on my skill a few years ago and was on a downhill slope…in more ways than one. About halfway down the mountain, I stopped to watch Peyton…and to rest at the side of the slope. As I looked down the slope, something slammed into me from above. I found myself on my back, knowing my head had taken a hefty blow on the hard snow and I thought I must have bitten both lips. *"Dang, that hurts!"*

I started to move my head and then thought I would take that opportunity to rest a bit longer as the sky was swimming before my eyes. My mouth was filling with blood, so I had to raise up on one arm. Colin was there and the snowboarder who had hit me was there asking about my well-being. *My being wasn't feeling very well,* but I assured them I didn't think anything was broken. Colin grabbed a handful of snow and I pressed it to my bleeding mouth. I instantly had what looked like a cherry red snow cone.

The out-of-control snowboarder apologized again and wanted to help, but I couldn't think of anything he could do, so he went on down the mountain.

I was thinking I could ski down, when the ski patrol arrived. They asked me questions, some of which took me a while to answer. I don't know if that was due to the whack to my head or the age I had to be to get the free lift ticket.

Regardless, they insisted they ski me down in their basket. *That wasn't on my bucket list!* I had skied for fifty years and never had to be taken down by the ski patrol. I was now officially a *basket case.*

Peyton was frightened by all the blood and I quickly assured her...as best as I could through cut lips and with a fuzzy head...that her Mimi was fine.

On that memorable ride down the mountain, I realized my teeth were just not fitting together quite right. Indeed, whatever had hit me in the mouth had pushed my front teeth back. The ski patrol medic called a dental office, and off I went to spend the rest of the day going from the dentist to the orthodontist's office in Boone to get braces on my upper teeth.

We were scheduled to come back home to the flatland of Wilmington the next day. I got to drink my breakfast, lunch and dinner as my mouth was a swollen mess. I definitely looked like I had lost the fight.

No matter how bad I looked or felt, I was glad I had gone to the mountain. We had made some great family memories and it was a birthday I won't forget. I was happy to mark two items off my bucket list, though the dental bills have far outweighed the price of that *free* lift ticket. Watching little Peyton was priceless and I was thrilled to have been there with her and extremely grateful I had been the one hit and not her.

I always learn something when I go to the mountains and this time was no exception. I am not too old to ski down the mountain. However, my body doesn't recover as quickly when I am old enough to ski free. Thus, in the future, I will be the senior ski bunny waiting in the lodge with cookies and hot chocolate.

"Life is 10% what happens to you and 90% how you react to it."

— **Charles R. Swindoll**

ED HEARN was born in Nashville, Tennessee on June 26, 1949 and lived there for his first fifty years. After graduating from college, he worked for a manufacturing/printing business for thirty years and served as a part-owner.

He has two boys, John and Matt, and two grandchildren, Owen and Isabella. The decision to retire came for Ed almost two decades ago, and he currently lives in the Landfall development in Wilmington, North Carolina.

Ed enjoys golf, tennis, boating, fishing, traveling, writing, creating highly detailed sculptures made of wood and bronze, producing acrylic paintings and participating in Masters track and field competitions throughout the United States and around the world.

He has been writing his entertaining and thoughtful short stories for the past few years in an effort to share his colorful life and varied experiences with both his extended family and other interested individuals.

The motivation for him to write and express his feelings in the form of short stories and memoirs was the result of his telling family stories during numerous family get-togethers. They were repeated many times through the years to everyone's enjoyment. He didn't want them to be lost to future generations and finally decided to sit down and create an extensive collection of his often humorous and interesting memories.

There are also additional stories about his reflections on life in general as an adult person. These are different in that they are more thoughtful and hopefully contain a bit of wisdom along with a degree of his philosophy about life.

MY FIFTIETH HIGH SCHOOL REUNION
Ed Hearn

When I was ten years old and preparing to enter the fifth grade, my Mom took a job as a dorm mother in charge of sixty boys in the ninth and tenth grade at a very unusual and unique kind of school in Nashville, Tennessee. My parents, two brothers, sister and I moved into a small apartment within that large dormitory building.

We arrived in 1959 and at that time the school contained about seven hundred children from the ages of six to about eighteen, both girls and boys. That included individuals from the first grade all the way to the twelfth grade.

The school had been started in 1885 and was funded by the state of Tennessee. The children were placed in the school by the juvenile court system so they would have a place to live, plenty to eat and a place to go to school.

The families involved were viewed by the courts as being in need of financial help and assistance for the benefit of the children. Usually, those families were missing a father or a mother from the family unit, who normally provided discipline and care. In some cases, this included an entire family of brothers and sisters, or in other cases, just one individual from a family.

Most of the children never went home throughout their years in the school once they arrived, even during the summertime. As a result, all the kids became one big family and were assigned to large dorms across the extensive campus where the guys all lived at one end and the girls lived at the other end.

My personal experience of growing up there was unique in that I had my parents with me daily and could go to them for emotional support and encouragement. The other students were basically on their own from the time they first arrived and lacked the important relationship I had with my parents.

In my opinion, the toughest part of the whole arrangement for the kids was that everyone became somewhat institutionalized, because everything was provided throughout all the years they lived and went to school there. We did everything together including going to two main cafeterias three times per day for food, going to elementary and high school together as large groups, assembly for church on Sundays, movies on Saturday night and attending sporting events on campus.

Because of that completely different way of existing as young kids, they all became very close emotionally. Eventually they graduated and were expected to go directly into the real world, get a job and figure out how to make a living. All the reunions in future years were seen as real homecomings and special. I graduated from that school and on my fiftieth reunion; I was going home to visit a lot of my friends from years ago.

I entered the building set up for the reunion not knowing what to expect. I was quickly involved as I moved through the crowd. I gazed into eyes I had not seen in over fifty years.

The question from a few was, "Do you remember me?"

My frequent response was, "Give me just a second to think."

Many times, on that special night of my fiftieth high school reunion, I was able to recall a name from years ago after carefully studying the individual's face, which was now covered by wrinkles and a head full of gray hair.

Sometimes I had to politely say, "Please give me a hint or at least a first name."

After that was done, I usually experienced an immediate recognition of the person who had been an important part of my past. Most everyone in the room had been one of my childhood friends in varying degrees. Some were recognized by me after first hearing their voice and others were identified because they still looked something like their old selves.

Many of my close friends I recognized immediately, and we quickly engaged in conversations about our current lives.

As I walked around the room filled with previous classmates, I could not help but go back in time and see each person in my mind as they had appeared during the years while we were still teenagers.

I was drawn to each person with great interest and was quick to ask questions like, "Where do you live now?" "What has been your job since high school?" "Are you still married to the same individual you first married?" "How long have you been retired?" Their answers to my questions were all absorbed by me with great interest.

Those I talked with but hadn't seen since graduation were the most fascinating. What they had done with their lives varied completely from person to person and I listened intently as they shared their experiences. In my head, fifty years had gone by in a heartbeat as I mentally traveled back in time with each one to the world I had long forgotten.

After all the introductions and the original questions, we sat in a large group and began to share stories from the time period during which we had grown up together. Everyone remembered those happenings from their own viewpoint, and they seemed to recall old events in their own special way. There was much laughter and joking among the group as we listened and responded.

A few of the stories that were told were quite funny, while being sad at the same time. An example was a story about a time just a week before graduation, and it involved the class of 1966. A small group of senior guys decided to sneak out of their dorm in the middle of the night and go visit the senior girls' dorm on the far end of the campus.

They had already worked out the visit with certain girls in advance, and a ladder extending to the second floor had been put in place. Upon reaching the dorm, they climbed the ladder and went through an open window to gain access. Quickly, they moved through the hallway to particular rooms containing their individual girlfriends to enjoy the night.

Somehow, the adult student supervisor, who lived on campus, had been alerted and he suddenly appeared in the main hallway on the second floor with other reinforcements. They began shouting for those visitors in the rooms to come out and identify themselves. That wasn't about to happen, so the guys began to jump out of the windows to the ground in the dark. There was yelling, screaming and quite a bit of pandemonium as everyone exited in an attempt to not get caught. That was the funny part of the story. Some were hurt while hitting the ground and ended up limping back across campus to get to their own dorm.

Those involved eventually confessed and the penalty was that they were not allowed to graduate just a week later. They had to leave the campus without their graduation certificates, nor were they allowed to go through the graduation ceremony. For a couple of them, that meant that even fifty years later, they still had never received their high school graduation certificate. For me, it was depressing to hear that news from a couple of those individuals present at the fiftieth reunion.

We later talked about the teachers who had taught us various subjects, the coaches who had been in charge of all the athletic teams and old classmates who were not present for the reunion. What had become of them? Did anyone know? We followed that discussion with story after story, including new information to process that carried me back to my days of youth.

There was also a short discussion included about those classmates who had died over the years. As the information was given, it was difficult to process, but very interesting and emotional. With those details about different individuals, I found myself thinking back about my past interactions with each one discussed, and the last time I had seen them.

The entire group mostly laughed and kidded each other throughout the evening. It was a wonderful time of reflection and the stories told were mostly full of humor. In fact, I soon discovered that I had laughed so much my cheeks were sore and new smile lines had appeared at the edges of my mouth and eyes.

At the end of our time together, we shook hands and gave big hugs all around, vowing to be present at the next year's reunion. In my mind, I knew it might be the last time I would ever see some of them. I also realized that, beyond question, they had all been a big part of my life during my critical early years.

While driving away, I began to think about my current age and my adult life. The simple realization came to me that our early friends are definitely very important in regard to who we ultimately become. All of those relationships carry on throughout our lives even though we may never see the people again.

At the conclusion of that evening, I originally felt a little sad, but later felt very happy to have been allowed an opportunity to be with them, and also to have a chance to reflect back on the "good ole days." Maybe I'll be able to do it again in the future, but I'm sure it will not be quite the same as on that night, which was my fiftieth high school reunion. I left knowing that I was really glad I had taken the time to attend.

A SPECIAL ENCOUNTER
Ed Hearn

My mind is at peace as I enter this familiar place of escape and all of my senses are tuned to the moment. I'm suddenly aware of the weightlessness of my body as I begin to float across the surface of the crystal clear, cool saltwater. I feel the warm sun on my bare back but most of my focus is directed below.

While gliding slowly through the water above the shifting, beige colored sand, I can't help but notice the many beautiful coral heads everywhere that are surrounded by intensely painted reef fish. The only noise I hear is the soft rhythm of my own breathing in and out through the short plastic snorkel attached to my glass face mask.

Where am I? I've just entered the water off the northwest shore on the island of Maui in Hawaii. I've been to this spot before; the last outing many years ago left me with wonderful memories of the nearby reef life. Named Black Rock because of the coal-black tinted cliffs forming a peninsula that extends out into the ocean about an eighth of a mile from the beach, it was formed by an ancient lava flow.

Rounding the outermost point of this isolated landmass in about fifty feet of water, I peer down through the depths and observe a large oval shape rising directly toward me from the bottom. My heart beat increases as it approaches because I am completely by myself, far from the beach, and I'm not immediately sure if I am in danger.

As the object gets closer, I identify it as an adult green sea turtle of about three feet in length. It passes me on the left side and surfaces within an arm's length from my face. As I glance sideways, its large dark eye stares directly at me. The intelligence it possesses is obvious and I rest my extended left arm on its broad floating shell and look directly into that right eye fixed in my direction.

For the moment, we are uniquely connected. There is no fear between us and I realize how special it is to be here with my new friend. This is followed by a long silence between us with no movement until suddenly the spell is broken by a quick turn of its body, a duck of its large head and a dive toward the bottom.

As quickly as it appeared, it is now gone. I realize that what I have left is the knowledge of a special encounter that will not soon be forgotten.

This type of experience is part of the reason I enter the ocean and snorkel with all its varied creatures; I never know what to expect on the next outing. Life in general is like that, also. Sometimes I have to go forward with no real expectations and hope that I am pleasantly surprised. On this day, I have been lucky enough to take with me another very positive memory and I hope my new friend agrees.

WHY AM I STILL HERE?
Ed Hearn

A few years ago, my mom was nearing ninety-two-years old. She had become bed-bound and her health was going downhill quickly. I traveled almost seven-hundred miles to be with her during what I thought might be her final weeks and was sitting at her bedside when she awoke early one morning.

She looked up at me with weak eyes and asked the question, "Why am I still here?"

With all the hope in the world for her recovery, I replied, "It's not your time yet."

She thought about that for a moment and said, "Each morning I wake up and realize that I've lived a full life. My days are short and I'm ready to go."

These words have stuck in my head now for a long time. As I look back, she was preparing her mind for the inevitable and I was having trouble adjusting to it.

During my last visit, we discussed all kinds of things, mostly about years ago when I was a little child. Her memory was very clear, but her body was old and worn out. She talked about things our family had done together when she was much younger and healthy.

She said, "I love life and I love my family."

"I know, mom, and we all love you."

After about another hour of discussion, she said, "I'm

getting tired now and need to sleep a little while to regain some of my strength."

"You know, mom," I reminded her, "that I must go back home tonight, but I will see you again in just a few days."

She nodded and said, "Take care, and I love you."

Shortly after she fell asleep, I returned to my home in another state and wondered how much longer her body could hold up. She was not eating well, getting no exercise and growing weaker by the day. I felt very bad about not staying with her constantly at that point, but knew I had to carry on with my life because I had no idea how much longer she would survive. My plans were to go back that following weekend to stay for an additional few days.

However, I received a phone call two nights later from one of the ladies who was paid to stay with her around the clock.

"Your mom asked me to get you on the telephone," the woman said. "She thinks she is dying."

Then, whispering into the phone, the helper said, "Your mom's hands and feet are turning a light shade of purple, including her knees. If things don't improve quickly, I will call an ambulance and have her taken to the hospital."

I knew instinctively that my mom's internal organs must be shutting down and not allowing blood to flow freely to her extremities.

I didn't know what to say, but she gave the phone to my mom and mom spoke slowly to me.

"I want you to know that I love you. I love my entire family including my daughter, three sons and my husband of over fifty years. I've enjoyed being with all of you as you've grown up and we did things together as a family. I think I'm dying and I wanted to talk with you one more time."

I didn't know what to say as tears formed in my eyes. All I could think to say was, "I love you too, mom."

There was a short silence and she then said, "I'm getting tired now and I need to hang up."

The phone went dead and I just sat staring at the wall. I knew that the chances of her living through the night were slim. I went to bed and woke up about four o'clock in the morning. The phone conversation came to my mind instantly and I said a little prayer to God. *If you must take my mom tonight, take her gently and in peace.*

I then went back to sleep and slept until eight o'clock the next morning. Shortly after waking, the phone started ringing and it was my younger brother, who was with my mom.

"Mom passed away during the night in her sleep. It must have been around four o'clock because the lady staying with her had just checked on her moments earlier and said she was breathing slowly, but asleep."

I thought about the timing of my prayer during the night and the estimated time that my mom had passed away. She had gone in peace.

Within a few hours, I was packed and on my way by car to be with my family. Since my dad and older brother were both already deceased; my younger brother, sister and I handled all the arrangements for the funeral.

During the drive, I thought many times about mom's

question to me, "Why am I still here?"

Maybe it was so she could give me that final call on the telephone where she expressed her feelings about her long life and her love for everyone in the family. I was glad I got that last phone call.

A DAY AT CASCADE PLUNGE
Ed Hearn

"Come on, Ed, let's go swimming today!" my older brother shouted across the room one sunny morning during the early summer of 1963.

He liked to include me in his adventures and I loved it. I quickly replied, "I'm in! Let's go!"

The approval for our outing had already been given to him by both parents, so we gathered two towels, suntan lotion, sunglasses, our bathing suits and a little spending money. We were out the door in a matter of minutes and on our way to a new place called Cascade Plunge.

That large public swimming pool was located about four miles from where we lived. It was warm outside and we had the whole day, so it didn't matter that we had to walk to get there. I was only thirteen and my brother was seventeen. We had both heard about the place, but had never been swimming there before that day.

With smiles on our faces and a day of fun ahead, we began our long walk through unfamiliar streets once we left our immediate neighborhood behind. I was glad that he had invited me because otherwise, it would have been a boring day.

My big brother was a strong athlete and a star football player with the varsity squad. He was a big and muscular person; I referred to him as "Charles Atlas" because of how strong he was at the time. I also looked up to him for being the trend setter in our family. He was good about pulling me into activities after he first tested them out. That particular outing would prove to be different in that it was a new experience for both of us.

We arrived around 10:00 in the morning and could hear music playing over the loudspeakers as we paid to gain access to the other side of the chain-link fence that surrounded the area. The smell of chlorine was strong in the air as we entered the locker rooms to change our clothes. After storing what we had been wearing in big wire baskets, attendants gave us a number on a metal pin so we could claim them later in the day.

Exiting the building, I looked out across the large, aqua-blue painted concrete deck in wonder. Many people were already swimming and playing throughout the pool. But it wasn't just any pool.

I saw a large slide and waterfall in the shallow end, and hanging five feet above the water were large metal rings attached to two-foot lengths of chain spaced four feet apart on a cable that spanned the width of the pool area. I watched one swimmer attempt to swing from one ring to the other across the pool; it looked difficult and I quickly decided to try it later in the day.

At the far end of the pool were two different diving boards: one being a standard low board and the other a high board, about ten feet above the water. I had never been off a board of that height, so I became determined to test my nerves and either dive or jump off of it.

In the middle of the two diving boards was a diving tower with wooden steps leading up each side all the way to two separate platforms at the top. The lower platform was separated from the higher one by a small trap door and as I looked, a boy climbed all the way to the very top and went through that trap door. He stood on the top level and looked out over the area before moving to the edge, where he looked down into the clear water below and jumped. The splash was big and he came to the surface smiling and laughing. I didn't know if I would have the courage to try the tower, but was eager to climb up there and at least look out over the whole pool area.

My brother decided to give the rings a try first and jumped off the side to grab the first one. He swung his body back and forth until he reached the second ring and then went from one to the other until he was almost to the other side. At that point, he dropped into the water but I'm sure he was strong enough to return on the same rings to where I was standing.

He shouted across the water to me, "Jump out and give it a go!"

I was nervous, but wanted do what he had just done. I leaned out and jumped toward the first ring only to find out that once my body weight was hanging from the ring by my hand, it was hard for me to hold on. I fell into the water and decided that I would come back later to try it again.

My brother then swam to the deep end and ran to the low diving board where he performed a cannonball. There was a big splash and I swam to the same area and got out of the pool. In order to outdo him, I climbed the ladder to the high diving board.

As I walked to the end and looked down at the water, my heart started racing. It was higher in the air than I thought while I was on the ground. In order to avoid embarrassment and prove I was as daring as him, I closed my eyes and jumped. Hitting the water took my breath away, but I had proved to myself I was not totally afraid of heights.

Next, my brother went to the tower and climbed about half way up to the lower platform that hung out over the water. This was about the same height as the diving board I had just jumped from. He leaned out and the next thing I knew, he was in the water and laughing loudly.

He said to me, "You've got to give this a try. It's not as high as you think it is."

I started climbing the steps as I didn't want him to kid me and say I was afraid to jump. When I reached the same step he had jumped from, I turned and jumped also. Wow! That was fun!

We both went higher and higher up the steps, testing one after the other as we jumped into the water. Soon, he became brave enough to climb all the way to the lower platform above all the steps and off he went. I was expected to then do the same. Although quite nervous inside, I repeated what he had just done. We were having a ball by testing each other to see who would jump from the highest level.

Next, he decided to go up and look down from the very top platform that was approximately thirty-five feet from the surface of the water. He crawled all the way up the steps and through the small trap door between the upper and the lower platform to stand silently looking down.

I hoped he would "chicken out" and not jump since I really didn't want to do it. Off he went into the water.

Darn.

It was my turn, and I was scared. Climbing the steps and

going through the trap door for the first time, I was shaking. As I reached the top and looked down, my knees began to quiver. I knew I could not go back down the steps without jumping; he would never let me live it down. I turned and jumped. As I hit the water, I was pleased. Now he could not make fun of me for being afraid.

Throughout the next few hours, we swam, dove off the diving boards and jumped off the tower. I even tried the metal rings and made it to the third one before my hands could no longer hold my weight.

We ate lunch at the snack bar and decided it was time to start the long walk back home.

He slapped me on the back and said, "I didn't know you were as brave as you have been today. I'm proud of you."

All I could say was, "Thanks," but his comment made me feel very good because I respected him and his opinion was important to me.

As we walked together, I was pleased that I had been invited and I was glad I had chosen to go with him. It wasn't but one year later that he moved away to college in another town and after that, I rarely saw him. Soon he was married and off on his own.

Never again did we share the same kind of fun we experienced on that special day at Cascade Plunge, but I always looked up to him with pride as my big brother. That day, so long ago, was a "coming of age" experience for me that I now look back on with fond memories.

A FUNNY MOMENT
Ed Hearn

During my college years, I participated in track and field activities across the United States. I very much enjoyed traveling with the other athletes on our team to various competitions, and we worked out with weights together almost every day while training.

My events were the shot put, discus and javelin. I had previously competed in high school with the shot put and the discus, so I was familiar with those activities, but the javelin throw was a new event for me in college. During my freshman year and after a lot of practice, the javelin throw became my premier event out of the three and helped me get into many major NCAA track meets around the country from 1968 until 1971.

In the late spring of 1970, I excitedly traveled to Ft. Campbell, Kentucky to participate in a large invitational track meet open to anyone in the United States. I went there with three other athletes from my school who were doing well in their running events. I planned to only throw the shot put and knew before participating that I would be somewhat out of my league with some of the other competition that would be present.

As it turned out, a world-class shot putter also decided to attend the meet. He had been working on a new technique he recently developed for throwing the sixteen-pound metal ball. It involved two quick, complete body turns in the seven-foot-wide concrete ring to increase speed before releasing the throw, similar to the technique used to throw the discus. The major rule was that the ball had to stay against the athlete's neck during the spin and then had to be pushed and not thrown with the arm. Up to that point, all shot putters had used a slide method to move their bodies directly from the back to the front of the ring, with no spin.

The new spin method of throwing had been approved by the national rules committee only a few weeks earlier, and that day's competition would be the originator's first time to actually use it. That man was Brian Oldfield—one of the biggest and strongest men I had ever seen at the time. I would guess he was six-and-a-half feet tall and weighed two-hundred seventy-five pounds. He was solid muscle and would have made a great middle linebacker for the Minnesota Vikings. Yet despite his large size, he was very quick. He could get from the back of the shot put ring to the front faster than I could blink my eyes.

The spectators for that particular track invitational were predominantly Ft. Campbell soldiers; close to 2,500 young men had recently completed training and were heading to Vietnam the next week. Most were between the ages of eighteen and twenty, and they all looked like kids who were supposed to be out playing baseball, not going off to war. The Army let all of them attend the track meet, so the stands on both sides of the field were totally packed. I had never participated in front of a full stadium until that day. It was exciting.

I noticed there was an official announcer on a loudspeaker located in the middle of the field. Everything was being handled very professionally with all the correct wind devices so that any world records would actually stand and be put in the record books.

The shot put event was scheduled to be one of the first

events and I approached it as usual by performing a lot of stretching and mental preparation to get myself ready.

I looked over at Brian and he was one mean-looking character; there was not a smile on his face. He started *his* warm-up ritual by doing a little screaming and then he began jumping up and down. That was all designed to pump himself up with extra adrenalin before the explosion needed to heave the sixteen-pound ball through the air.

I watched in amazement off to the side. He continued warming up by picking up the shot put, placing it in position against his neck and then pounding it into the ground at his feet. It had rained the day before and the ground was moist, so the ball penetrated the damp soil to a depth of about six inches deep. He would then dig it out with one big hand and wipe it clean with a towel before repeating the process. That guy was really putting on a show and the crowd loved it.

The announcer then said over the loudspeaker, "Everyone should be aware that at the shot put ring to the side of the track, there is a participant with us today who currently holds the third-best throw in the world. He is Mr. Brian Oldfield from Tennessee and that event is about to start."

All eyes in the stadium immediately turned to our area. Brian never acted like his name was mentioned. He continued to scream and throw the large metal ball into the ground as hard as he could. He was pumped. I glanced up again into the stadium and no one was looking anywhere but at the shot put ring. Everyone in the stands, all 2,500 of them, were now on their feet trying to get a better look at that monster of a man.

The loudspeaker announced that Brian Oldfield would be the first competitor. He stepped into the ring and seemed to be in a world of his own. He crouched in the back pushing the big ball to his neck with arms that looked to be the size of an average man's thighs. After a short wait to get ready, Brian began to scream again at the top of his lungs as he spun around the ring to build speed. He made two complete turns very quickly and the scream increased in volume.

The following explosion was so fast and powerful that I thought the ball had been shot from a cannon. Through the air it sailed, much farther than I had ever seen a shot put thrown in the past. Brian never stopped screaming and continued long after the ball finally hit the ground. I didn't know what to think.

The crowd was totally quiet and everyone was still standing as I looked across the stands. No one moved as the two officials met in the middle of the throwing area to have a discussion. One had a clipboard and the other had an official metal measuring tape. Together they measured off the distance while everyone waited for the result. Retracting the measuring tape, together they walked across the field to the loudspeaker booth where a small conference took place as the crowd waited in silence.

The loudspeaker finally came on with a loud squeak and the announcer cleared his voice. "Gentlemen, you are all very lucky to have been here today. You have just witnessed the best shot put throw ever in the world. The measurement of sixty-nine feet and four inches will be the new world record. Mr. Oldfield has beaten the old record by over a foot in distance."

The crowd went wild with excitement and everyone started clapping. Each and every person was cheering and became totally involved in the moment.

As the stadium finally got quiet after a few minutes, the surprising announcement came from the loud speaker, "Our next competitor in the shot put ring will be Mr. Ed Hearn."

I could hear off in the distance my teammates as they yelled, "Give 'em hell, Hearn!"

Of course, I gave it my best shot, but it did not come close to Brian's new world record. Later on, Brian and I became good friends and eventually he broke that world record three more times during his long and famous career.

One day in 1975, he threw the sixteen-pound ball seventy-five feet, but it was not counted as a world record because he was a member of the professional United States track team (a team that only existed for about four years). At the time, if you were a professional, your distance could not be counted as a new world record. That is not the case anymore.

My lifelong experiences with sports have been full of enjoyment and I have met a lot of great athletes, but this Ft. Campbell event stands out in my mind as one of the funniest moments I can remember.

MEMORIES OF MY DAD
Ed Hearn

Recently, I walked through our spare bedroom and for the first time in many years, my focus was pulled to a small black-and-white photo mounted in an old, silver-colored frame. Displayed on an end table beside the bed, the image captured a special moment sixty-three years ago, when I was only five years old.

It was a simple photo that showed me standing slightly behind my dad who was seated in his favorite chair in our small living room, with my left arm draped around his neck as I leaned toward him. In turn, dad was reaching up with his right arm to give me a hug. He was slumped down in the chair, which he usually did shortly after arriving home from a long day at work, but we were both smiling and looking directly into the camera.

The picture didn't show color, but he was wearing a long-sleeve, starched white shirt and blue industrial pants that were considered his "work clothes." The worn red leather of his old chair was badly wrinkled, and the cap I was wearing (my favorite at the time), was a two-tone dark blue and yellow, with alternating panels on the top.

As I looked at the photo, I could once again smell the scent of used motor oil coming from my dad's hands. He worked around metal parts in a large hardware supply store and the metal items were always coated with oil to keep them from rusting. His hair was still dark black at the time that photograph was taken, when he was only thirty-three years old; it had not yet become solid white, which was the way I remembered him most in his later years.

I stared at that old photo for a long time in deep reflection as if I had never seen it before. Many fond memories of my dad began to move slowly through my mind. He was a kind man who was devoted to his family and we all knew it. I remembered how much time he had spent with me over the years as we went hunting, fishing, boating and worked together on various projects around the house. He was always determined to teach me the correct way to get things accomplished. My dad was that way and he did it all with love in his heart.

He told me regularly, "I'm not always going to be here to show you how to do these things, so you need to watch and learn so you will know how to teach your own children."

Indeed, after I married and had two sons, I tried to pass along those same qualities I saw my dad give to me. Both sons have now grown up and are fine young men of whom I am proud.

That photo on the table quietly reminded me of the fact that time constantly moves forward and continually removes people we care about from our lives. Now, my dad has been gone for twenty-two years. I miss him.

I hope one day my sons will be able to look at an old photo of me and have the same positive feelings I experienced when I noticed that old photo with my dad...that had been ignored for so long.

BECOMING "THE HUNTED" WHILE IN AFRICA
Ed Hearn

For several years, I had thought of going to Africa to hunt for big game. Finally, I couldn't hold back the urge any longer and decided to arrange a two-week hunting trip in July 2008.

I called my younger brother, Jim, and asked him, "What do you think about going on a hunting trip of a lifetime with your older brother?"

He thought about it for only a short time before responding, "I definitely want to be included in that adventure—I wouldn't miss it for anything!"

Jim and I had hunted together when we were kids, but I assured him that the trip I had now planned was going to be far more exotic and dangerous than simply hunting rabbits in Tennessee.

After checking out the available game animals that could be harvested, we decided to hunt aggressively for some of the larger horned beauties of middle to southern Africa. Therefore, I scheduled a trip to Zimbabwe that had been recommended to us.

I then called Jim and told him, "The trip has been arranged and we are to have our own personal hunter. Together, we will push every action to the edge of our safety for a maximum experience."

"I'm excited and can't wait for the trip to start," he responded. "What do you think about us coming back with a few different species of animals each and have all of them mounted in the United States to ensure a high level of quality?"

"I think that would be a good idea," I said.

On July 2, we found ourselves on an almost seventeen-hour flight to Johannesburg, South Africa. I personally felt a lot like Indiana Jones as the airplane flew around the globe and we tracked our progress on a map of the world. It seemed amazing that one day we were at home and the next day we were in South Africa, halfway around the earth.

At the airport, we checked in with our host and personal hunting guide, Mack Jordon, who had been waiting for our arrival. We were both exhausted, but excited beyond belief and tingling with anticipation.

"I'm working out of the Hunting Lodge of Bulawayo, located near a small town in Zimbabwe," Mack explained. "It will take a few hours on bumpy roads to get there in my jeep, so let's get started."

Mack was built like a weight lifter and had skin like leather, so it was obvious that he had spent his share of the daylight hours in the intense African sun. It was also apparent that Mack was efficient in everything he did, including the careful handling of all our hunting arrangements down to the smallest details.

He began giving instructions during the drive. "I have guns for us to use and each rifle, with its high-powered scope, is sighted to within one quarter of an inch at one hundred yards. Each of you will also have a separate pistol that is to be strapped to your waist; I intend for you to carry it constantly as additional protection from unexpected threats."

Mack didn't talk much, but when he did, we learned quickly that you definitely wanted to listen. When asked a question, he provided a short but complete answer...unless the question came across as completely stupid to him, at which time he would give only a sharp look without a reply. Based on that, we decided to think through our questions before voicing them to that very serious man.

Our ride to the hunting lodge in his old, beat-up jeep was rough, to say the least. By the time we finally got to our destination many hours later, I felt like a rag doll shaken to the bone.

During the trip, Jim had said to me, "I think I'm getting a little car sick. This heat and the thick dust coming off the road are overwhelming."

I felt sorry for him and said, "Hang in there because we'll soon be at the lodge where we'll start having a lot of fun."

Upon arrival, we discovered the lodge was very basic, but had everything we needed. It sat upon a slight rise overlooking an open plain with unusual trees and plenty of flat land. The outside of the lodge was covered in brown field stone and the inside included beamed ceilings, wood floors and a big fireplace in the main room. There were three small bedrooms, two baths and an open kitchen with a large table and eight wooden chairs.

During the first evening, the temperature was about fifty degrees, so we did not require any heavy clothing. Mack made a campfire outside and we sat around it as we discussed plans for our very first hunt the next day.

"Be sure and remain close to me and don't venture out into the bush on your own at any time," Mack warned. "The lions are known to attack unexpectedly and will jump from the thick grass if they catch anyone by themselves."

That information immediately got our attention and later caused a constant state of anxiety.

He continued, "There are dangers from elephants, rhinos and even the hippos that usually hang out around the water holes. Those animals are known to charge humans without any advance notice. Just stay alert."

After Mack's vivid discussion about the major dangers of the area, we headed off to bed. We were to be up and ready to go at seven o'clock the next morning. I drifted off to sleep thinking about the unusual and exotic place we were staying, located completely on the other side of the world from our homes.

Just before full daylight, I was awakened by animal sounds in the distance and arose to see through the faint mist a herd of zebras kicking up a dust cloud about a half mile from the hunting lodge. Instantly, I was excited and ready to go.

I woke Jim and told him what was happening outside. We quickly dressed, ate some bread with a little fruit that was waiting for us in the small kitchen, and went outside to the open-top jeep to make sure we had all our equipment, including rifles, ammunition, and a good camera.

Mack came through the lodge door with a smile on his face. "Come on guys, I'm going to show you the real Africa."

The three of us, as well as two black men who worked with Mack, jumped into the jeep and we bumped down the dusty road just as the sun was about five degrees off the horizon. I was excited and ready for whatever lay ahead.

We drove for almost an hour on our way to the first hunting site. Along the way, we noticed there was plenty of open land with lots of grass and large spans of bare dirt, which was an orange-brown color. There were small trees and thorny, green bushes scattered everywhere across the open plain with clusters of thick, three-foot high, tan grass growing in large clumps. One small pond that contained dark, muddy water was passed on our left where a few small animals were coming in for a drink.

Mack stopped briefly and said, "Let's watch for a short while from a distance. It'll be fine for you to take some photos of the wildlife."

All the animals seemed to be in constant readiness around that small water hole, and I could tell that they would not hesitate to run if any threat came close.

After traveling for another fifty minutes, Mack stopped and said, "Get your gear from the back of the jeep and let's begin our walk through the bush to start your big game hunt."

The two helpers, named Itz and Meta, knew exactly what to do and they had everything unloaded and onto their backs within a few minutes.

Jim and I were handed the two rifles and told, "Go ahead and load your guns so they'll be ready as we walk."

On that particular day, the goal was to track and kill an aged gazelle or kudu, both of which would make a great head mount with their warm colors and beautiful, twisted horns.

We began to walk away from the jeep, all five of us, across an open area and entered a large grassy plain. In the distance, we could see animals moving. There were two giraffes towering above everything else and feeding in the tree limbs about a quarter of a mile away. Mack was vigilant as we walked and made sure that we were all together and that no one was lagging behind.

Through an opening in the grass, we could see a small herd of animals roaming toward the rising sun. I got out my binoculars to identify the species: gazelles! I was impressed by their beautiful colors of cream, brown, black and salmon.

Mack said, "Let's track them as they slowly walk toward the east. Be sure to crouch down as you move so your head doesn't stick up higher than the grass."

Itz and Meta didn't make a sound in their bare feet as they followed us with our gear through the dirt and grass.

Nevertheless, every time we got close enough to sight in on the gazelles, they would move aggressively to a new area about two hundred yards farther away. We found ourselves tracking those beauties for at least an hour, and I began to wonder if we had moved too far away from the jeep for our safety. Mack didn't seem to be concerned, so we all kept quiet and continued the hunt.

What we didn't realize as we moved toward the quarry was that we were not the only ones hunting. Mack was the first to sense that something was wrong. He quickly turned and motioned with his finger over his lips for us to stop and be completely silent. I was unsure what was happening, but I could tell he was concerned. He held his rifle out in front and slowly squatted down. Then he indicated for us to start backing up. As we moved, it was obvious he wanted us to move quickly and stay quiet.

After we had retreated about seventy-five yards, he stopped and whispered, "There are at least two lions crouched down in the grass ahead of us, waiting to attack one of the gazelles. They normally hunt in small groups so there could be more hiding close to the others."

Fear gripped me as he talked and sweat began to trickle down my forehead.

Unsure if we were safe enough to head back toward the jeep, Mack decided we should stay where we were, but to sit back-to-back in a circle with our guns ready in case the lions appeared from the grass.

We then heard a loud noise about seventy-five yards away and watched as one of the female lions bounded through the grass into the open as she chased a single gazelle that had foolishly wandered from the herd.

The female lions stalk the prey and normally are the ones who make the kill; the males wait around and feed as soon as the meal is on the ground.

The lion chased the animal for about twenty seconds in large sweeping circles, but somehow the gazelle avoided getting taken down. In one quick, final leap, it avoided the hungry lion and caused the lion to stop the chase. The gazelle then headed hurriedly in the direction from which the herd had disappeared. The female lion walked back in our direction to the grass, where I was sure there were others waiting for her.

My fear increased when I heard the noises made by the other lions as she entered the grass, not more than 150 yards away. Lions are known for their stalking ability and surprise attacks. It occurred to me that we might be in the process of becoming the hunted.

Mack whispered, "Don't move. Let's just wait to see what

happens."

I couldn't understand why he did not want us to back out of the area toward the jeep. When I indicated with my hand that we could go backward, he whispered quietly, "It's too far."

By Mack's hand and body language, in addition to the serious look on his face, we all knew he was deeply concerned. When I looked into the faces of both Itz and Meta, I could tell they were also scared. That didn't make me feel any better about our predicament.

Within ten minutes, the heat became almost unbearable. The sun had risen overhead and was beating down on us like a furnace. Jim was beginning to sweat profusely. His shirt was completely wet and dripping water from the bottom edges. I could tell he was now wondering why he had agreed to make the trip with me.

We had a canteen with fresh water that I sipped and quietly passed around. Just then, there was a noise in the distance that sounded a little like horses snorting, but it was far away.

Mack slowly raised his head to see and turned to us and said, "There are a herd of zebras approaching on the far side of the lions."

As the zebras moved closer, the African breeze carried their scent in our direction. They continued to walk directly toward the pride of lions hidden in the tall grass.

We could see two lions begin to crawl forward on all fours in the direction of the zebras. They seemed to always keep a stand of grass between themselves and the zebras as they positioned their bodies to attack.

As the herd of zebras approached the outer edge of the grass, one lone animal limped slightly away from the herd. In an instant, the two female lions jumped from the grass and started after the injured zebra.

There was a short chase, but the zebra was no match for the two hungry, aggressive lions. They leaped onto its back and had the zebra by the throat in a matter of seconds. The largest female lion did not let go with its choke hold until the zebra stopped moving completely. I couldn't help but feel sorry for the black and white animal.

To my surprise, a large male lion moved out of the grass in front of us, followed by two cubs for a total of five lions in the pride. If the zebras had not come along, they may have moved in on us. That was not a pleasant thought.

We watched in awe as the five lions converged on the downed zebra and began to tear into its gut. Red blood quickly covered the lion's faces and feet. They gorged themselves over the next thirty minutes.

The smell of the kill must have drifted out over the savanna because three African spotted hyenas appeared out of nowhere. They stayed a short distance from the zebra on the ground, but slowly began to pester the lions. Their hunger must have been overpowering because they pressed their safety to the edge. Closer and closer the hyenas pushed until finally the lions moved away back to the grass, but only after letting the hyenas know they were unhappy by growling repeatedly. The lions repositioned themselves in the heavy grass while the hyenas took over the kill.

Mack whispered to us, "Stay put at this location and remain

ready with your rifles."

The heat was stifling with only a light breeze that, as bad luck would have it, suddenly began to shift. Instead of us being downwind where the predators couldn't smell us, we were suddenly upwind. As the lions looked in our direction, we ducked tightly to the ground. We knew it would not be long before they would check out our location.

Mack indicated with a quick motion of his hand for us to stay low and move back in the direction we had come. All five of us slid across the African dirt on our stomachs as swiftly and quietly as possible. I knew that our scent, mingled with sweat and fear, was being carried directly to the lion's nostrils.

We could almost feel the lions moving in our direction through the dense grass, as we backed away slowly. I was sure they were approaching from different directions, based on the way they normally hunt.

Mack wore a look of fear on his face. Itz and Meta were visibly trembling. My only comforts were the rifle and handgun that I carried at my waist.

As we eased away, we slowly lost the cover of any grass and found ourselves out in the open. I didn't know if that was good or bad, but Mack indicated for us to move faster in the direction we were going.

The three hyenas, also alerted by our smell, were the first to appear to the right side of the grass and cautiously move toward us.

Mack stopped and said, "Get ready for an attack."

We positioned ourselves close together with the rifles all pointed in the same direction. I decided that I was going to take out at least one of the hyenas if they moved toward us very much farther. They were showing their teeth in an aggressive manner, and I could tell we were in for some serious trouble.

Suddenly, to the left side of the grassy area, one of the female lions appeared. She seemed to ignore the hyenas as she also came toward us slowly with teeth bared.

Mack was the first to react. He shifted directions, lifted his rifle and sighted on the female lion. I decided that I would address the hyenas. Jim also focused on one of the hyenas and in unison we all fired three single shots. Down went the female lion in a screaming fit and instantly, two of the three hyenas were on the ground. The third hyena disappeared in a fast run in the opposite direction.

We didn't move and remained ready for whatever was to happen next. Everything remained quiet and I could feel sweat dropping off my forehead and onto my cheek. I was so scared that I was trembling. Fear had its hold on me and I wasn't sure if I could aim correctly if I needed to shoot again.

We waited in a tight cluster for at least fifteen minutes before moving. Slowly, Mack raised himself up and moved toward where the female lion was lying on the ground.

He motioned for us to follow and said to us, "Keep your rifles ready in case the other lions have not moved away."

He checked the lion to see if it was dead by bumping it with his rifle barrel. There was no movement and I began to relax. Mack moved slowly into the grass to see if the other lions were still waiting. He became convinced that they had been scared away with the gun shots and we all relaxed.

Mack then told us, "This is the closest I have ever come to being actually attacked. We were lucky."

After resting and recovering for a few minutes, he said, "The female lion and the two hyenas will make beautiful, full body mounts to remind you of this close encounter."

Mack decided to send both Itz and Meta back across the African plain to get the jeep so we could load up the three animals. After approximately forty minutes, we could see another small group of zebras moving in our direction. Since we were still located behind the grass in a seated position and the breeze had again shifted in our favor, the herd slowly got closer and closer to us.

Mack leaned over and whispered, "Do you want to shoot one of the older male zebras in this herd to add to your trophies? Shooting a male zebra is not easy and sometimes involves days of hunting in order to get close enough."

Jim quickly said, "Why not?"

We watched the zebras get closer and closer. Mack picked out one of the larger and older males that stood in front of the group, within one hundred yards of where we sat. I knew Jim could hit it squarely in the shoulder for an instant kill, and I let him lay the rifle barrel across my left shoulder so he could aim more carefully. When the zebra glanced in our direction, he pulled the trigger. It was a perfect shot and the animal went down immediately. Again, I found myself shaking because of the excitement of what we were encountering on that day.

Mack and I turned and shouted, "Congratulations!" as we both gave him a high five.

We ran out to see the zebra that was now lying by itself. It was a perfect specimen and Mack again explained, "The male zebra is not easy to obtain even though there are many herds of zebras traveling across the African landscape. The females are much more plentiful. I picked out a very old male that would soon die for you to shoot."

Mack, Jim and I sat with the lion, the two hyenas and the male zebra for another two hours until we heard two vehicles approaching in the distance. Itz and Meta pulled up in a cloud of dust with the jeep and another open bed truck was following. We found out they had radioed the lodge that we had made a kill, and two other fellows from the lodge had driven out the open-bed truck in order to easily transport all our trophies from the field.

It didn't take the four men long to load the female lion, the two large hyenas and the male zebra.

I told Jim, "They'll all make beautiful mounts."

Jim responded, "Yes, these animals are fantastic. Look at the beautiful fur and the long claws on the lion along with the hyenas' large teeth. The zebra is also awesome with the white and black stripes. Our taxidermist will be excited to have the opportunity to mount them. These trophies will serve as great reminders of our exciting African adventure."

After one last look at the four animals, we all jumped into the vehicles. As we rumbled over the bumpy ground, I looked over to discover Jim had a big smile on his face. I could tell he was glad he had come with me to Africa, even though there were plenty of doubts earlier in the day.

As the lodge came into view, the evening sunset was

outstanding. There were a few clouds hanging low in the sky and the warm evening sun filtered through them in shades of pink, gray, blue and violet.

What a day it had been! We originally came to Africa to hunt for big game and take home animal trophies, but we had underestimated the dangers. I learned on that day an important lesson: Sometimes the hunter can actually become the hunted.

A MEMORABLE MOVIE
Ed Hearn

By chance, I recently watched an old movie on television that made me start thinking about my life. This has happened to me with other movies that contain special lines of conversation or a specific theme that I reflect on for years. If you've seen it, you will remember it.

In this particular movie, *Life or Something Like It*, Angelina Jolie portrays a popular and attractive newscaster who thinks only of herself while rising rapidly in the news and broadcasting industry. After finishing a live morning interview on the streets of New York, she passed an old prophet verbally revealing his visions of the future while standing on a box.

Through a quick conversation as she passed him, he told her that she would die that week on Thursday. This caught her by surprise, but she passed over the comment for the moment. Later in the day, she began to think about what he had said. She remembered that he had also predicted that a particular football team would win the afternoon game by six points. While sitting in a bar after work with a friend and watching the game, she saw this come true. At that time, she began to feel anxiety and developed a great fear that she might really die on Thursday.

Since it was early in the week, Angelina had a few days to consider her life. Everything began to take on a different meaning. She began to see how superficial and unimportant most of her life had become while she had focused mostly on herself each day. She then began to struggle with the thought that maybe her life would soon be over and realized how little had been accomplished of real importance. Every moment became precious while an effort was made to tell those close to her that she loved them. She also apologized to others for the way she had treated them in the past.

In the middle of the day on Thursday, Angelina found herself in the wrong place at the wrong time. While observing the arrest of a criminal, she sustained a serious gunshot to her side during a random accident on the streets of New York City. On the operating table, her heart stopped beating and she quit breathing, but surgeons miraculously revived her. This proved the earlier prophet correct in his prediction, but she had survived the tragedy.

As a result, from that moment on, her life totally turned around. She became a different person who was very thoughtful and only involved herself in meaningful undertakings in service to other people.

The moral of this well-done story was easy to observe and absorb. It was stated clearly at the end of the movie in one short sentence: "Live your life as if every day is your last, because someday it will be."

I walked away from watching this movie with a new and fresh understanding about the correct way to live each day. It reinforced my feelings that all our moments are important, precious and limited. The greater lesson, which was also obvious, was that we need to live each day so that when we look back on our lives, there will be no regrets. We need to learn to use each day to create good memories for ourselves, so that when we grow old, there will be a great and lasting peace deep within our souls.

A BUCKET LIST MOMENT
Ed Hearn

I had always wanted to run in a ten-kilometer road race. It was one of those things I had on my bucket list, but realized I needed to train and prepare sufficiently before actually doing it.

During December of 1979, one of my friends who was in charge of recruiting participants for a race asked me, "Would you be a part of a special benefit road race to help me out this coming Saturday morning? The route you will be traveling through is surrounded by open, rural farm land and is quite beautiful. The event will cover the full distance of six and two-tenths of a mile."

I knew there would be a number of very experienced and serious runners entering the race, but also there would be a lot of weekend joggers. I expected many people to drop out of the race after starting because of their lack of preparation and the long distance.

My friend then said to me, "If you get tired, you can just stop."

Since I am a very competitive person and had wanted to enter one of those races for a long time, I said to him, "Yes, I'll do it to help you out, but I'm a little nervous about it."

Having been a very physically active person for many years in high school and college, I was aware that a distance of over six miles would push me to my maximum at my present level of fitness. The next afternoon, I took a watch and started jogging around my neighborhood at a slow pace to see how fast I could run and keep going for at least six miles.

Starting off very slowly seemed to be the best course of action. Only after four miles, was my pace increased, and it seemed like I needed to travel about a mile every twelve minutes to be able to finish in just a little over one hour. My plan was to pay attention to my watch while running and to run no faster than that speed. I had no extra time to prepare before that coming Saturday morning, so the decision was made to enter the race just to finish.

Early Saturday morning, the weather turned really bad. It was cold and raining very hard. I traveled to where the race was to start, and was unsure if it would actually still take place. There turned out to be only a small group of die-hard runners who chose to run in the race because of the unexpected bad weather. What I was not prepared for was the extreme lack of inexperienced runners like myself. It seemed that the people at my level had all decided to stay home, or at least chose to not be a part of the event at the last moment.

As I looked around, the other participants were wearing the latest clothes and shoes right out of the latest running magazine. I was dressed in an old, baggy sweat suit that was at least ten years old and a pair of regular tennis shoes. The serious runners were busy doing stretching exercises and meditating in preparation of the run, because the race was scheduled to start within fifteen minutes.

Soon, the starter assembled everyone in a large room and discussed the route to be taken through the countryside. He said, "There will be an ambulance following behind the very last runner just in case anyone in the race develops a serious problem."

Immediately, I wondered if the ambulance would bother me, but decided it would probably be a long distance behind everyone during the race. That turned out to be wrong.

Everyone lined up on the starting line with the rain coming down heavily. The gun fired and off we went down the main street. I stayed near the back of the pack so I would not hold up anyone who was determined to have a fast start. I had no more than rounded the first turn in the road when the realization hit me that I was taking up the rear. Everyone had started very fast at almost a sprint for the first quarter of a mile. That was not my plan, and I was determined to not be intimidated.

While glancing down at my watch, which helped me set my pace, the sound of a motor took my attention from behind. Turning my head, I noticed the ambulance was no more than three feet behind me and traveling at the exact speed I was running. There were two guys in the front seat, so I threw up my hand and waved to acknowledge I knew they were there.

After the first mile my legs were getting tired. My face was probably getting a little red from the activity after the second mile, because the driver of the ambulance leaned out the window and through the rain said, "Hey buddy, do you feel okay?"

He then added insult to injury by asking, "Do you want to climb in and ride to the finish line?"

That really got to me. I knew how out of shape my body was, but I didn't realize it showed so much. I lowered my head in the rain and replied, "I came to finish this race and I'm doing just fine."

The driver continued to follow just behind my heels and

was driving me crazy. It made me feel as if I was doing so badly that he was expecting me to fall over at any minute.

About every additional mile, the ambulance driver would again ask, "Are you sure that you don't want to jump in and ride to the finish line?"

My answer was always the same, "I'm planning to finish this race."

We passed through some very small country roads surrounded by farmland. There were many barns with cows and horses lining the wire fences that bordered the road. Up and down the hills I jogged and the rain kept falling so heavy that I could hardly see. It seemed like my clothes weighed a ton.

The nearest runners ahead of me were at least a quarter of a mile away. I set the goal in my mind to at least catch and pass the closest person before we reached the finish line. After five miles, I realized three of the runners were falling behind the pack and were getting closer to me. There might be hope after all. I picked up my speed gradually, but the ambulance continued to follow within a few feet.

The three runners turned out to be two girls and a guy, and they were now no more than a hundred yards ahead with a mile left in the race. I was determined to catch them or die. Picking up my speed even more, I closed the gap and even began to pull up beside one of the girls. It was all I could do to get my breath, and my body was exhausted by that time.

Off in the distance, the finish line began to come in to view. I could tell the runners who had already completed the race were standing to the side of the road and cheering for everyone else, as we neared the finish line. By that time I had passed one girl and one guy, and had begun to feel good because I knew I was not going to finish in last place.

Down the final stretch we ran. Having pushed so hard to catch up with the last two runners, I was beginning to run out of gas. I still had a chance of not being last. The guy I had just passed suddenly showed some renewed energy and blew by me in a sprint.

The girl was beginning to pull up beside me, and I considered tripping her to slow down her progress. I found myself in a footrace down the stretch and all the other finished runners were cheering. Running as fast as I could, the last girl ended up beating me by a nose at the finish line.

I walked away feeling embarrassed, but remembered my goal at the start. It was only to finish the race. By looking at my watch, I realized my overall time had been much better than expected.

There was a big celebration inside for the winners after the race. Trophies were awarded to the top men and the top women in different age groups. While hiding in the back of the room near my friend who had invited me to the race, the man in charge announced, "We also have a prize for the person who finished last in the race."

My name was called out, and I was asked to come to the front of the room so the presentation could be made. There he stood with a small basket of flowers.

As he handed them to me with a smile on his face, he said, "I can tell you are a good sport so we will make the presentation in spite of you being a man. We were certain that the person who would come in last would be a woman who would like flowers."

My friend never let me live down that crazy award. The following day I started exercising and began a weekly jogging program. During the next few years, I successfully ran in many other similar races, but never again finished anywhere near last place.

That day's experience had served to motivate me, and I was definitely glad I never stopped to get in the ambulance.

MY MOST UNFORGETTABLE INDIVIDUAL IN SPORTS
Ed Hearn

During the early summer of 2009, I decided to start participating in Masters track and field sports after a gap of thirty-eight years, since I had last participated in that activity while in college. I had heard about the nationwide Masters track program sponsored by the United States of America Track and Field (USATF) and decided I would become involved.

First, I joined the association by using the Internet and then bought a new javelin, shot put and discus. Within two weeks, I traveled to Oshkosh, Wisconsin where I became part of the season-ending United States Masters National Track and Field Championships during the first week in July.

While attending that large competition, I met an unusual person who had just enjoyed his ninety-fifth birthday and was competing in six events. His name was Leland McPhie and he lived in southern California. Leland was a likable person with a soft-spoken voice and I could tell he was a highly driven athlete. He was not big and strong due to his advanced age, but he was intense in attitude. Leland was quick to smile and didn't mind being asked questions about the sport he loved.

Only one other person (who had also just turned ninety-five) was in Leland's age bracket and his name was Max Springer. Max was also a very talented athlete and that made for great competition against Leland. In the Masters category at the major events, all the athletes compete against other competitors who are within their five year age bracket.

The first event for the day was the shot put. I watched intently as Leland proceeded to throw the iron ball farther than any man had ever thrown in his age bracket. His new world record on that day was twenty-two feet six-and-one-half inches while using a seven pound iron ball. I was amazed as I realized what was happening. Afterwards, the local television station had a camera available and a reporter interviewed him for the evening news.

When all the excitement was over, I walked up to Leland and began to talk with this interesting man. He told me that he had competed for most of his life in track and field, going all the way back to high school and college, and would soon be long jumping against Max Springer in his age bracket.

I wanted to watch that event, but was unable to do so, due to the fact that my main activity of the javelin throw was to happen at exactly the same time. I told him that as soon as I was finished, I wanted to come by to see how he had done.

Two hours later I walked up to him and asked, "Well, how did you do?"

Leland responded jokingly with a big smile on his face, "I beat that old guy by one foot in distance!"

I laughed at his statement and shook his hand while giving him my congratulations. He had just long jumped six feet and five inches at the age of ninety-five years old.

I asked Leland what event he would be doing next and was told it would be the high jump. I moved quickly to the high jump area in the stadium and got a good seat up front. It wasn't long before Leland began to do some practice jumps. The bar was originally set low at about thirty inches, but I remembered this was a very old man I was observing. He easily cleared that height and the final competition quickly began.

The bar was moved upward in two inch increments until it reached three feet and two inches, which was the previous world record for anyone over the age of ninety-five. The stadium got very quiet as the announcer stated over the loud speaker that a world record was about to be tied at the high jump pit. After a slight hesitation, Leland made his run-up, leaped and cleared the bar. The crowd went wild.

He had tied the old world mark and was determined to now break it. The bar was then set at thirty-nine inches. As a large gathering of spectators grew around the high jump pit, the announcer stated that history was in the making. Sure enough, Leland cleared the bar for a brand new record on his first attempt. This was his second world record of the day.

I went over to congratulate him and saw a big smile appear on his wrinkled face. He remained humble, but I could see the pride he held within himself as a result of that accomplishment.

He went on to successfully complete three other events that day and I watched them all. Those included the discus throw, javelin throw and the triple jump. In these three events he finished short of world marks, but they were outstanding for a man of his age. As he left the stadium in the afternoon, I noticed he had six gold medals around his neck and a fresh bounce in his step.

We became good friends and I would later visit him at many events around the United States and the world over the next five years. He told me that he didn't have any good photographs of himself participating and asked if I would take a few and send them to him at his home in southern California. I did this on numerous occasions and once received a nice letter back from him thanking me for what I had done.

I last saw Leland participate during a big world track and field competition while he was ninety-nine. When I heard that he would be long jumping, I had to see it. I first observed how much he was slowing down from four-and-a-half years earlier when we had met in Wisconsin. He was moving slower, but still had the same competitive spirit. While sitting in the stands on that hot afternoon, I watched my hero jump almost five feet to win the event. When he left the meet, he was wearing a gold medal around his neck and a big smile on his face.

The next time I heard from him was just after he turned 100 years old. In the springtime of that year, he attended the United States Masters Indoor National Championships in Boston as a competitor in three events. While there, he was honored with a lifetime achievement award for the many years of his involvement in track and field. Throughout his life he had experienced many victories, but had remained a humble person who was always a pleasure to be around. I admired that man.

I was saddened to hear a year later that Leland had passed away at his home after his 101st birthday. He was the type of athlete that I strive to be: competitive until the end and admired by all. I will miss him in the future, but his memory will always be with me. He will remain my most unforgettable individual in sports.

ACHIEVING MY LONG-TERM ATHLETIC GOAL
Ed Hearn

As I began sprinting down the rubber runway in my spiked throwing shoes, I could feel a strong rush of powerful adrenalin pumping through all my muscles. My senses were keen and alert. I pulled the long spear completely backward in my right hand and focused on a target in the blue, cloudless sky. My final few steps were covered at top speed and I was prepared to explode with maximum energy.

Looking skyward, I instantly realized I had executed a perfect throw because the javelin flew straight and long before it finally touched down well beyond the distance thrown by any of my competitors. Quickly, the officials ran to mark the spot and then electronically measured for the outcome in meters.

My distance was broadcast loudly as a full forty-five meters and I was thrilled with that result. From past experience, I knew that a legal throw of that length would be difficult for any of the other competitors to surpass.

For months I had worked long and hard to physically and mentally condition myself to be at my very best for this World Championship event. I now realized that my commitment and sacrifice had been well worth the effort.

Within the next hour, and after all the different athletes from various countries had put in their final six attempts at passing my mark, it was announced that I had won the competition by almost seven feet. Countless emotions surged through my body, for my ultimate goal of winning a World Title in my Masters level, five-year age bracket, had now been finally achieved.

At sixty-seven years of age and with memories of long ago when I first distinguished myself as a victorious collegiate athlete, I reminded myself that I "still had the touch." A peaceful moment, quiet and surreal, enveloped me as I stood tall and proud with both arms extended to the sky in personal thanks and triumph.

The thrill of the moment lingered for me as we all shook hands and offered congratulations. I then gathered my belongings from the large tent that was setup in the middle of the stadium in Daegu, South Korea. This was the 2017 World Masters Track and Field Indoor Championships and I was truly overwhelmed by my accomplishment.

The three top finishers were then escorted to a waiting limo that carried us to the main stadium about a mile away. At that location, we were all led to a three-tier award podium for the celebration and presentation of our individual certificate and medal.

Since I had won the treasured gold medal, the American flag was displayed behind me on the top platform of the podium. On the second level of the podium was the flag of Estonia and my new friend, Lembit Talpsepp, who won the silver medal. And finally, on the third level of the podium was the flag of the Czech Republic and another new friend, Vladimir Srb, who won the bronze medal. By being the winner in that presentation, the national anthem of the United States was to be played just after the medals were draped over all three of our heads and hung proudly around our necks.

While standing at attention and as the music began; I placed my right hand over my heart and looked out across the crowd before positioning my eyes on one additional American flag to the left, front side of the podium. The American national anthem was then played and I actually felt tears forming in my eyes as I quietly sang along with the song. I was determined to retain the special memory of that event in my mind long into the future.

After the music stopped and the ceremony concluded, I stepped down off the platform and soon realized I was a changed person with a more humble attitude as I walked through the crowd. There were smiles everywhere as I passed the many observers. That day and that achievement will never be forgotten.

AGING TOGETHER
Ed Hearn

On a recent trip, I sat at a quiet dinner table and enjoyed a conversation with a nice couple who were a few years older than me. I discovered they had been married a long time and they told me their current outing had been on their bucket list for many years.

As I sat and listened to an overview of their lives together, I knew they had been through much change and challenge as they raised their children, worked their jobs and finally retired. They seemed content and happy about how things had turned out for both themselves and their children.

Our conversation finally focused on life in general and how true the statement is that life truly becomes what we make it. We discussed that there are many things out of our control daily, but our decisions and attitudes have a huge effect on the person we become and how we then influence those around us.

We talked about aging while still feeling young mentally. They seemed to be a good example for how best to live, so the last part of life would be enjoyable. We realized that to have a partner with us in old age who views everything in a similar way would be a gift that not all of us share.

What I gained most from that experience was a personal desire to continue on the path I am now following and to surround myself by examples like that couple. They were having fun, doing activities together and growing older each day in a way to be admired. There was a strong sense of peace about them that was obvious in their lives and relationship. I left them after our short visit and determined in my mind that I wanted that quality in my own life.

To be able to smile at everyone you meet, enjoy new people and relationships while creating lasting memories would be worthy goals for a successful life. I relearn those basic principles each day and value what it does for me internally. I would recommend sharing any of those thoughts with everyone you encounter each day.

It's a wonderful world in which we live and you never know how much our actions and conversations influence those around us in positive ways.

AN EVENING OF STAR GAZING AND REFLECTION
Ed Hearn

A few nights ago, I sat alone on a warm evening and stared upward at the dark heaven above. I could sense the air surrounding me was very still and I could see that the sky was clear and black, revealing only an occasional cloud to hide the numerous stars overhead. The brightest white spot, and the one I focused on first, was the planet Venus. It was easy to find using nothing but my eyes. I was then able to locate Mars, which is easily identified because of its slight orange coloring due to the strong iron content in its soil.

My mind began to drift and I had meaningful thoughts about the vastness of space and the relatively small size of planet Earth, in comparison to everything else. I remembered some technical information found recently on the Internet that stated the closest star, other than our sun, is approximately 4.2 light years away from us.

Since light is known to travel at 186,000 miles per second through the vacuum of outer space, that places the closest star of Proxima Centauri at 24.64 trillion miles into the distance.

I also recalled reading that the fastest current technology for an unmanned spacecraft would allow a maximum speed of 40,000 miles per hour. Based on those figures, it would take 91,000 years or approximately 3,033 generations for humans to travel to our next closest star, if using modern technology.

Those are overwhelming numbers that our minds can hardly comprehend, but they show the vast distances involved in our entire universe with all its billions of individual galaxies.

With that in mind, I then shifted to thinking about the huge expanse of our universe in relation to my individual existence within it. I began to look into the star-filled night sky, with all those facts running through my head, and couldn't help but feel humbled. I thought about the entire scope of things and considered, in my smallness, "Can I really be all that important?"

The realization then came to me that I possess a consciousness of my surroundings that exceeds all other creatures. I had to conclude that the answer was, "Yes, I am definitely important." Without my intelligence allowing me to observe the magnificence of creation and realize its full value, surely everything would be a different reality and my individual importance would be totally changed.

I looked even deeper inside myself on that enlightening night with all those additional insights and it gave me a sense of calm. I knew that if I reflected on everything in the correct way, my life was truly valuable with a true purpose and that bit of knowledge alone gave me a strong reason to be alive.

One more thing I also began to realize, as I sat there in the stillness, was the fact that much can be gained by simply being quiet on a summer night, while staring up with an open mind at the stars.

"The past beats inside me like a second heart."
— **John Banville**

Dr. Richard J. Nasca was born in Elmira, New York. A graduate of Georgetown College and Georgetown Medical School, he is a retired orthopaedic and spine surgeon. Dr. Nasca held teaching appointments in orthopaedic surgery at the University of Arkansas School of Medicine and the University of Alabama School of Medicine. During his time in practice, he specialized in caring for patients with spine deformities, injuries and disorders.

He has been married to Carol T. Smith, RN for fifty years and has three children and one granddaughter. He lives in Wilmington, North Carolina where he is a volunteer with The Good Shepherd Center for the homeless and at the Cape Fear Clinic.

Dr. Nasca is a certified Master Gardner and is a member of the University of North Carolina Wilmington Life Long Learning Program. He is serving on Advisory Boards at the College of Health and Human Sciences at UNCW, and has served on the Landfall Foundation Board, Landfall Men's Golf Association Board, and coached with the First Tee of the Greater Wilmington Area.

He has published two children's books (*Paul Pro T* and *Tommy Tomato*, available on amazon.com and blurb.com), coauthored *Medical Malpractice: How to Prevent and Survive a Suit* by Data Trace Publishing Company, and has contributed short stories to *Pieces of Life* (available on amazon .com and blurb.com).

GOING TO THE WOODS
Dick Nasca

I grew up in southeast Washington, DC in a row house a few blocks south of the Anacostia River. Between the river and our street was a large park, Fairlawn Park, fronted by thick woods paralleling a railroad track. Fairlawn Park had ball fields, a golf course, swimming pools and the Boy's Club. My friends and I spent many hours playing sports on the fields, learning to swim and going to the Boy's Club.

For Christmas one year, I received a large red wagon with side boards. I would fill the wagon up with pieces of wood I had collected and a few tools and head down the street and across the railroad tracks to the woods leading into Fairlawn Park. Some of my buddies would come along and we would build forts, tree houses and observation posts using the scrap lumber we collected. Some of the tree houses were large enough for us to use for our secret meetings, accessible only to those who possessed a Sky King Decoder ring (obtained by sending the top of a Corn Flake box to Kellogg's in Battle Creek, Michigan).

One day, my mother got mad at me for being disobedient. As I tried to run away, she lashed me with the Hoover vacuum cleaner cord. I was so upset, I decided to load the wagon up with some clothes and food and run away to the woods. My plan was to live in one of the tree houses and not return home. The Boy's Club nearby would provide shelter during bad weather as well as water fountains, bathrooms and showers. I planned to cook out over an open fire.

It was getting late in the day when I finished adding a roof to one of the tree houses and began gathering some firewood to cook up some soup and hot dogs. After dinner, I went up in the tree house, looking forward to a nice, quite night away from home.

To my surprise, I was greeted by a family of skunks who had decided to make their home in the tree house. When the skunks saw me, they became very agitated and started to growl and shake their tails.

With great haste, I grabbed my clothes and food, tossed them in the wagon and headed home. It was dark and the doors to our house were locked so I spent the night on our porch.

The next morning, my mother found me asleep on the front porch, not because she saw me, but because Mom had a keen sense of smell. You guessed it: I had been sprayed by a skunk. My clothes were burned and it took several days for me to get rid of the odor.

DORMY
Dick Nasca

Each year, we have a Ryder Cup competition at our golf club. This consists of four nine-hole matches pitting two people on one team against two on the opposing team. The second of the four matches is the modified alternate shot. Both team partners hit their drive and then you play your partner's tee shot and he plays yours. After that, you alternate shots until the ball is holed in the cup.

On the first hole, my partner Dan almost hit his ball out of bounds. Luckily, my drive ended in a good spot and we were on the green in two putting, thanks to a nice shot by Dan. For the first two holes, we matched scores with our worthy opponents, Dave and Gary.

On the third hole, I hooked Dan's tee shot through some bushes hoping, it went through. He hit my tee shot into some trees. Things were looking grim until we found my errant shot had cleared the bushes and was nestled down in the deep rough about seventy yards from the pin. Dan hit a flyer over the green, which landed on a high mound overlooking the green.

Our competitors in the meantime had positioned themselves for a birdie putt. They won the hole and we moved on to the fourth hole, being one down in the match. We lost the fourth and fifth holes. Our opponents were hitting the greens with laser precision and making birdie and par putts. We were now three down with four holes to go. In order to stay in the match, we needed to at least a tie on the sixth hole, a par three over water.

Dan and I both hit shots onto the green and were able to make par for a tie. We were now three down with three holes to go: a condition described as *dormy*. We needed to win the next three holes in order to tie the match. That was a real challenge since our opponents were playing so well.

On hole seven, my partner hit his ball in the water. My drive in the fairway was about 110 yards from the pin across water to an island green. Dan hit my ball onto the green. We made par and our opponents just missed par due to an errant putt.

On the eighth hole (a par five), we were on the green in three...as were our competitors. We made par again to win the hole.

We faced a stiff wind coming directly at us as we teed off on the ninth hole. Dan hit his tee shot into a fairway sand trap. My drive was short, so Dan had to lay up rather than go for the green. In the meantime, our opponents hit one of their second shots into the water in front of the green and the other near a stand of trees in the deep rough.

I was able to get out of the fairway bunker with a shot close to the green and Dan got on the green. We finished with a bogey and our opponents a double bogey to tie the match.

One dictum in sports, especially golf, is to never give up because the momentum of the match can change in an instant. You are often rewarded for persevering and staying the course.

MISSING ON CALL
Dick Nasca

Each year, the Hospital of the University of Pennsylvania appointed forty medical graduates from around the country as interns to staff its 1,000-bed hospital at 34th and Spruce Street in West Philadelphia.

Interns were divided in to three categories: rotating, surgical and medical. There were twenty-four rotating interns who were dispersed to spend a month or more at each of the various hospital departments, services and clinics. The eight medical interns spent most of their time in medical clinics and medicine floors, whereas the surgical interns were involved with duties in the operating room and on surgical floors and clinics such as general, cardiovascular and thoracic surgery.

At night, the interns were on duty from 6:00 PM to 6:00 AM to cover the entire hospital. We were on call every other night and weekend. We would meet after supper (around 11:00 PM) to exchange information and divide up the requests for our services. In 1964, there were no beeper pagers or cell phones; we were paged over the hospital's public address (PA) system by the operators who took calls from the floor nurses in need of our services.

As I recall one autumn evening, there were four of us on call. Kevin was a surgery intern, as was Barbara. Bob and I were rotating interns. Kevin was a tall, athletic guy who exuded confidence and quick response times. He was always punctual and did a good job on his assignments.

The wards were unusually quiet, that evening, so we all headed off to our rooms to catch a little sleep until we received the inevitable call from the hospital operator. About 3:00 AM, I got a call asking if I had seen Kevin since he was not answering his calls. I told the operator I last saw him around midnight. She instructed me to go to the general surgery ward to hang some blood, which I did.

Around 5:00 AM, I returned to the intern quarters and noticed the red light on the phone was blinking. I called the operator who told me Kevin was still not answering his pages. Security had been dispatched to find him.

Rather than go back to bed, I showered, changed clothes and went down to the cafeteria for breakfast. On my way, I noticed security near one of the hospital's service elevators. As I approached, I was surprised to discover Kevin stretched out on the elevator floor, fast asleep.

Twenty years later, I ran into Kevin at an orthopaedic meeting where he had presented a paper that was well received. After I congratulated him on his presentation, we chatted and I learned that he was also in an academic orthopaedic practice and happily married with children in high school. We also shared a good laugh when Kevin recalled being found asleep on the service elevator.

MY VICTORY GARDEN
Dick Nasca

As you might recall, during World War II, the U.S. government rationed sugar, butter, milk, cheese, eggs, coffee, meat, canned fruits and vegetables. Labor and transportation shortages made it difficult to harvest and move fruits and vegetables to market, so the government encouraged citizens to plant "Victory Gardens."

Slogans such as "Our Food Is Fighting" and "A Garden Will Make Your Rations Go Further" were popular. They wanted people to provide for themselves. People brought seeds and dug up their yards and vacant lots to make their Victory Gardens.

Meat was rationed, so you needed to save a number of little round, red coupons before you could buy beef and pork. You saved metal tooth paste tubes, wire and tin cans to recycle. Automobiles, bicycles, garden and hand tools were in short supply.

In the spring of 1944 when I was almost six years old, my mother came home with several seed packets. She encouraged me to make a Victory Garden in our yard near the back steps that led into our rented row house in southeast Washington, DC.

My Dad was working for the American Telephone and Telegraph (AT&T) in downtown Washington, DC. He was rarely home because his work involved setting up communications and providing transmissions for our armed services.

My next-door neighbor and friend, Ernie (age ten), and his sisters had already planted a small garden. Since I didn't have any garden tools, I asked him if I could borrow some of their tools. Without any hesitation, he handed me a rake, shovel, pitchfork and a very small metal hoe.

The dirt was mostly red clay and was very hard to dig up. After several tries, I finally broke through the surface layer and got down a few inches. It was getting late in the day when my other next door neighbor, Frank (a chief petty officer in the U.S. Navy Band) came over to lend a hand. In a short time thanks to Frank, I had a 4 x 8-foot plot of yard dug up.

As we stood admiring our work, the air raid sirens went off. We quickly dropped everything and ran up the street to the air raid shelter in the basement of the Fairlawn apartment building. After a few hours, we were released to go home. Mom and I ate a late supper in our dark kitchen with the shades drawn down.

The next day, I got up early to resume my digging. I found the little metal hoe to be the perfect tool to pulverize the big chunks of red clay. As I was working the hoe, I noticed Ernie's six-year-old sister Gail staring down on me from their back porch.

A few minutes later, she came over to where I was working and grabbed the hoe out of my hand. She let me know that I had no business using her hoe. A fight ensued and I ended up with a deep hoe cut across the bridge of my nose that required a trip to the hospital.

A week after my injury, I ventured out into the backyard with my own new little rake, shovel and hoe. I planted radishes, carrots, lettuce, beets, and beans in my little garden.

My best crop that year were the radishes.

NIGHT ON THE TOWN
Dick Nasca

It was a hot morning in early July of 1967 when I arrived at the orthopaedic outpatient clinic. As I looked at the list of patients scheduled for the day, I noticed that a VIP was scheduled for an admission to the hospital that afternoon. I asked the head nurse if she had any information on the person, but she did not have a clue.

After lunch, a tall, young, muscular man was called to the admissions office. Since I was the senior resident, I was told to get him worked up for surgery the following morning. I sent the intern up to do the history and physical and write the admitting orders.

Around 4:00 PM we got a call that the VIP (a NFL quarterback) who was admitted for surgery on his throwing elbow wanted to leave the hospital to have dinner with friends. After granting his request, the staff instructed him to return to the hospital later that evening and to not eat or drink anything after midnight.

Around 5:00 AM the next morning, I got a call from the hospital nursing supervisor that the VIP quarterback had not returned from his "night out" and that my boss (the division chief) was furious. I quickly got dressed and tore off to the hospital in my VW bug.

As I walked up to the ward, I saw the VIP quarterback tiptoeing down the hall and enter his room. A few minutes later, our team with the chief surgeon appeared. The chief surgeon had cared for the quarterback during his college days and knew him well.

The surgeon told him that there was no way he was going to operate on him in "the condition he was in" and that he should pack his bags and go home. The quarterback got down on his knees and pleaded that he be operated on so he could salvage his career, claiming that his painful elbow prevented him from throwing an effective pass.

The chief surgeon looked him in the eye and said, "In your condition, I can't operate on you under general anesthesia."

The quarterback again pleaded for surgery saying, "I'm afraid I'll be cut from the team if my passing doesn't improve.

The chief surgeon instructed us to get the quarterback to the OR. A few minutes later, we prepped his multimillion-dollar throwing arm for surgery under Novocain, a local anesthetic.

A few months later, the VIP quarterback led the NFL in passing stats and had his best season.

PASSING THE TUBE
Dick Nasca

I was a junior medical student rotating through general surgery at my university's major teaching hospital when I was assigned to see one of the private patients of the chief of surgery. The patient, a middle-aged man, had been admitted for an intestinal obstruction.

I was instructed to place a Miller Abbott tube to relieve the obstruction. This consisted of tying a bag full of mercury to the tip of a very long plastic tube, lubricating the tube and passing the tube through the patient's nostril into his pharynx and esophagus. The patient was extremely cooperative and the procedure went off without difficulty.

I went about my other duties, completely forgetting the passing of the Miller Abbott tube. Around 4:00 PM, I heard the hospital operator page medical student Nasca to the Department of Radiology *stat*. When I arrived in the X-ray department, the chief of surgery, chief of radiology and supervising surgery residents were there viewing X-ray films.

The chief of radiology pointed to a film with a bright metallic image on it. It was a flat plate X-ray of the patient's abdomen showing the mercury. There was another film taken earlier of the same patient showing the same metallic image.

The chief of surgery than asked me to describe what I was seeing. I indicated that the metallic object was the mercury bag attached to the Miller Abbot tube and that it had moved down the intestinal tract. What I did not say was that the bag of heavy mercury had passed though the obstruction which would remove the need for the chief of surgery to operate on the patient.

On one hand, I felt triumph for relieving the patient's obstruction and on the other, concern that the chief of surgery had been upstaged by a third-year medical student.

The next day on rounds we visited the patient who was doing well. I was instructed to remove the Miller Abbott tube, which I did without difficulty. The patient expressed his thanks for my efforts that had enabled him to avoid surgery.

A few months later, I was invited to an afternoon cocktail party at the home of one of my former high school classmates. To my surprise, I noticed that the chief of surgery was there. My friend told me that he was a close friend of his father and that he lived in the neighborhood. I tried to keep my distance, but after a short time, my friend's father took my arm and headed over to speak with the chief of surgery.

The chief, holding a freshly poured drink, reached out to shake hands with my friend's father as I stayed in the background. A moment later, I was nudged forward to greet the chief by my friend's father who then disappeared into the crowd of guests to enjoy conversation in the sunny backyard.

When the chief asked me what my future plans were, I mentioned that I was interested in surgery and mentioned a few specialties that I was considering. He turned to me, put his hand on my shoulder and whispered in my ear his recommendation that I apply to surgery programs in the northeast and southeast, which had more to offer me in the areas of my future career interests.

A few months later, I was called to the chief's office to pick up his letters of recommendation to several prestigious medical centers in the northeast and southeast.

SHEPHERD'S PIE
Dick Nasca

Yesterday was vegetarian day at our local Good Shepherd Soup Kitchen. Each year, a family sponsors a vegetarian meal and this year's selection was Shepherd's pie.

We cooks replaced the ground meat with ground-up baked mushrooms and added sautéed onions, celery, and peas, topping the mixture with mashed potatoes and cheddar cheese. It tasted very similar to Shepherd's pie made with ground beef.

This triggered the memory of the circumstances surrounding the best Shepherd's pie that I have eaten. My wife and I were spending a month in Killington, Vermont in a two-bedroom condominium near the Killington ski slopes. Across from our condo was a nice indoor pool with a hot tub, which we would frequent each day.

One day, we saw a young athletic man working out in the pool with a physical therapist. As it turned out, he was spending two weeks in Killington and staying in the unit below ours. After introducing ourselves to him, we learned that he was a professional rugby player and the captain of the Irish Rugby team in London. He had come to Killington to receive blood product injections and physical therapy for his arthritic knees.

We invited him to our condo for dinner and he spoke about his girlfriend and his parents. He mentioned that he would probably retire after the coming season because of his bad knees and start coaching or return home to Dublin and join the family business. He mentioned that he liked to cook and offered to cook dinner for us.

To our surprise a few nights later, he brought us a large Irish Shepherd's pie casserole that he had cooked using his mother's recipe. He used chunks of lamb rather than beef, freshly cooked peas, carrots and creamy whipped potatoes topped with Irish cheddar cheese.

I am sure it was his mother's Shepherd's pie that later got him the head coach's job with the Irish Rugby team in London.

SIDEWALK ROLLER DERBY
Dick Nasca

There were a number of boys and girls who had clip-on skates in our neighborhood. These were the kind of skates that attached to the sole of your lace-up shoes. You used a key that you wore around your neck to tighten the clips of the skate to your shoes. We would skate on the sidewalks and streets.

One day, while watching our black-and-white fourteen-inch Dumont TV, my friends and I saw *Roller Derby*. Teams skated around a circular track. To keep the lead, the lead team would prevent the challenging team from passing by setting up blocks using two to four skaters. With persistence, the challengers would somehow get ahead of the defenders on high-speed curves. Then the passing team would set up blocks. The sport got pretty rough as skaters threw body blocks and bodies flew off the track.

My friends and I decided that we would try our own version of Roller Derby, which we named "Sidewalk Roller Derby." The track consisted of a series of sidewalks that ran through the neighborhood. In order to compete, you had to learn to navigate the sidewalks, jump the curbs and enter the streets while racing at top speed. Body blocking was prohibited.

Races lasted around fifteen minutes. Finishing without falling was an accomplishment. After a race, there would be a time out and another race would begin. Once in a while, your skate would fly off your shoe and you had to retrieve it and put it back on. When this happened, you were most often out of the race and could not catch up.

As Sidewalk Roller Derby became more popular, we transitioned to an asphalt parking lot at the local junior high school. Using chalk, we made a circular track with lanes. People from the surrounding neighborhoods came to compete. We added body blocking and limited the race to ten laps. The most exciting time during a race was the passing. Usually, your teammate created a hole for you to accelerate through by blocking out the challengers. You had to be quick and fast since the opportunity to move ahead was short lived. During the winter months, we would move to buildings with large basements and set a track around the structure's supporting pylons.

The best part of the day was the after-race parties with cupcakes, ice cream and hot gingerbread cake with fresh whipped cream.

NEIGHBORHOOD MEMORIES
Dick Nasca

Our neighborhood of row houses in Anacostia was located in Southeast Washington, DC about eight miles from the U.S. Capitol. We were in close proximity to schools, churches, stores, and the Anacostia Navy Yard and Air Station.

My next-door neighbor Frank was the bandmaster for the U.S. Navy Band. Another neighbor, Harry, was the lead flutist in the band. Every week or two, several of the band members would come over to Frank's or Harry's house to practice. During these jam sessions, the neighborhood was filled with Sousa marches and other patriotic melodies to the delight of the residents, who often took time to sit on their porches to listen and watch as we kids paraded up and down the sidewalks.

Birthday parties were often elaborate affairs. Neighbor kids of all ages were invited and the mothers went out of their way to provide plenty of home-baked cake and ice cream. We all got dressed up in our Sunday best and came with nicely wrapped presents.

Another treat was the arrival of the Good Humor Ice Cream truck during the summer months. You could hear the jingle of the truck's bell as it entered the neighborhood. All the kids would grab their money and rush to get in line to buy their favorite dairy treat. The "ice cream man" was dressed all in white with a black bow tie.

Vanilla ice cream coated with thick, dark chocolate on a stick was my favorite. It cost ten cents and on warm days, it melted fast and needed to be consumed quickly. If we we missed the Good Humor truck on our street, we would run around the neighborhood to catch up with it before it sped off to another neighborhood.

Two or three times each summer, a large open truck came around the neighborhood loaded with watermelons. These were grown on farms in southern Maryland, a few miles south of Anacostia. Sometimes, the driver would sell them for twenty-five cents, but he often gave us kids a melon or two to take home. Before eating, we plugged the melon to taste it and then put the melon in the refrigerator to cool it down. In the fall, he brought pumpkins for Halloween.

Our row of houses was on the flight path to the Anacostia Naval Air Station. During the Second World War, Navy fighter planes would fly directly over the roofs of our houses as they were preparing to land at the Naval Air Station a few miles away.

The noise from the engines was deafening. The planes came so close to our houses that often you could see the pilots sitting in the open canopies of their planes as they prepared to land. We all got used to the planes and were happy that they there to protect us.

Air raid drills were another experience for our neighborhood during the War. Initially, it was a frightening experience, but after a few drills it became less so. We would all run up the street to our designated shelter in the basement of a large apartment house when the sirens went off. Once there, we would get out the army cots and thick, coarse wool blankets, the water and food supplies and set up the tables. The drills usually lasted a few hours and ended when the all-clear notice sounded. We were all happy to return to the comfort of our homes.

SLIPPERY SLOPE
Dick Nasca

My wife Carol learned to snow ski as a young child. Each winter, she and her family would travel to Vermont from Philadelphia to ski at Mount Snow. I met Carol in the fall of 1964 during my internship at the Hospital of the University of Pennsylvania. A few months later, she asked me to drive her to the airport for a ski trip to Kitzbuhel, Austria and Garmish, Germany. During the ride to the airport, she inquired whether or not I had any interest in skiing. I indicated I would give it a try.

Shortly after she returned from her ten-day ski trip, she arranged for us and another couple, Kay and Jim, to go to Elk mountain in the Poconos for a day of skiing. Jim was a fellow intern at Penn and an experienced skier, as was Kay. I was instructed to rent a pair of skis, poles and boots for the day. I was a bit taken aback when I was told that the ski package would cost $25 for a day rental. Considering I was making $90 per month, that was a chunk of change. Not wanting to appear to be a piker, however, I dutifully rented the skis.

Carol had us show up at her apartment at first light of day for a full breakfast. After breakfast, we loaded the skis and poles on top of Jim's car and headed up to Elk Mountain. It was a sunny and cold day. It had been rather warm the day before. When we got to Elk mountain, I noticed more ice than snow. Jim assured me that he would get us to "some good snow that I could handle."

However, in order to get to the lifts and the good snow, you had to first walk over a lot of thick patches of ice. Needless to say, I did not fare well on the ice attached to the skis. I kept slipping and falling. I never did make it to the lift and the good snow. Jim suggested that I take off the skis and rest up while he scouted for some good snow with Carol and Kay.

About twenty minutes later, the three of them returned. The scouting trip produced no favorable snow, just a lot of ice due in large part to the previous warm day followed by a very cold night. It was decided to abort the trip return to Philadelphia. On the way into the "City of Brotherly Love," I dropped off the rental package expecting a refund for the early return and the sparse use of the equipment. That did not happen.

For our Christmas present in 1966, Carol's parents sent us two tickets for a one-week ski trip to Gray Rocks and Mount Tremblant, about eighty miles north of Montreal. At the time, I was working as a first-year resident in orthopaedic surgery. Before I left for the trip, my mentor called me in and cautioned me to be safe. He told me that if I came back in a cast with a broken leg, that would be the end of my orthopaedic career.

The plan was to meet up with another couple from Penn in Montreal and the four of us would drive together to the ski resort. While waiting for them to arrive, Carol took me shopping for ski pants and a jacket in downtown Montreal where the clerks spoke more French than English. I was finally outfitted with a pair of tight ski pants and a warm ski jacket with a lot of zippered pockets.

When we arrived at Gray Rocks Inn, there were over 300 people signed up for the ski classes. Carol was placed in Class 2 and I in Class 30. My instructor was a former women's downhill skier for the Canadian National Team. She was in her sixties and very fit.

On our first morning, the temperature was five degrees below zero when we started. After three hours, I came in for lunch soaked with perspiration due the fact I had too many clothes on and the drills she put us through. For three days (morning and afternoon), we did uphill and downhill drills, which consisted of walking up the hill and snowplowing down to a stop. We also did lateral walking and traversing to build up our legs. Finally, on the fourth day, she took us up the lift for a short ride over the hills we had been climbing the past three days.

Our class of ten people all got on and off the lift without difficulty. We had a great time riding up the lift and snowplowing down. On the fifth day we got to ride several lifts and were shown how to make a stem turn. Once we learned to turn the skis, we could go down some green and easier blue trails. On our last day, the class was taken over to Mount Tremblant for a trip to the top and a ski down the winding mountain. Due to our preparation and training, we all made it down without difficulty.

That night, Class 30 was called up to receive our certificates, which read "Novice Skier." Carol's class was called up to receive their certificates that read "Expert Skier."

Encouraged by my "achievement" at Gray Rocks, Carol made sure that one or two ski trips were on the agenda for the next thirty years.

THE WHITE LINE
Dick Nasca

I was in my junior year of high school in the spring of 1955 when our track team received an invitation to participate in a southeastern regional track meet at the University of North Carolina, Chapel Hill. I was very excited to be included and was looking forward to "going South." I had never been south of Northern Virginia.

My teammates and I boarded a Greyhound bus at the New York Avenue station in Washington, DC. We headed for the seats in the back of the bus, which gave us plenty of room to spread out. When we got to Richmond around noon, the driver announced we would have a forty-five-minute lunch break before departing for Durham and Chapel Hill.

I remember we had a great lunch of roast beef, mashed potatoes and green beans with apple pie for dessert. I also remember the signs saying *White* and *Colored* bathrooms.

As we were boarding the bus, we went to the back where we had sat before. The driver made an announcement that we were to move up front, forward of the *white line* painted on the floor of the bus. We did not respond to the announcement. A few minutes later, the driver came back to our seats and told us to move to the front of the bus immediately. However, our teammate Robbie, a light-skinned Afro-American was told to stay in the back of the bus. The bus rapidly filled up with colored passengers as we made our way to the front seats with our travel bags.

We arrived in Chapel Hill around mid-afternoon. After a briefing, we were sent off to our accommodations in a large gym filled with army cots. We put our gear under the cots and made our way down to the outdoor track that surrounded the football field. After that, we took a walk through the campus and enjoyed our dinner in the large cafeteria. There were only white athletes at the dinner.

    The next morning, after a rather uncomfortable night on the Army cot, our team went down to the track for some warm-ups before breakfast. Our meets were scheduled for late morning and mid-afternoon. I was to run the 60 and 100-yard dash, and the second leg of the 4 x 200-yard relays. The 60-yard dash was a blur of black bodies passing me at great speed as I followed them to the finish line. I made it through the first heat of the 100-yard dash, but was beaten out during the second heat by a muscular black boy. Our relay team did well, with Robbie running the final lap in record time. We just missed getting into the final heat in the relay.

    When it came to crossing the white finish line, those relegated to the back of the bus were first.

"We do not remember days, we remember moments."
— **Cesare Pavese**

Marie Varley Gillis is a graduate of Forsyth School for Dental Hygienists, Northeastern University, the University of Maryland at Baltimore, and NOVA Southeastern University. As Dental Hygiene faculty, program director, and Infection Control officer, she was employed at Howard University, College of Dentistry for fifteen years. In addition, she has more than twenty years of clinical practice in periodontal settings. She was employed by Education Affiliates as the National Dean of Dental Programs for twenty-eight dental assisting and seven dental hygiene programs.

Currently, she is self-employed as an educational consultant for accreditation issues, curriculum development, and continuing education programs through Dental Academics, Inc. Her future endeavors include teaching online courses for dental hygiene programs as well as teaching interdisciplinary practice courses in the online doctoral health science program for Nova Southeastern University.

These stories are her first ventures into writing fiction.

IT'S ALL ABOUT THE BROWNIES
Marie Varley Gillis

It was a comfortable and stylish brick, center-hall colonial with ample land for my boys to explore in suburbs of Providence. They were ten, eight, and six years old at the time. Our lives were in turmoil after the abrupt departure of their father, and I was struggling to keep the house while coming to terms with the realization that would not be the case for very long. Every dollar was marked for a bill and there was no room for luxuries or waste.

However, I tried to keep our routines as normal as possible, in spite of going from part-time to full-time employment. It was important to keep them active in scouts and sports. Accordingly, it was my turn to provide the snacks for the afternoon meeting of my oldest son's cub scout gathering at the local elementary school the next day. I decided on the family-preferred homemade brownies—a particular favorite of my individual scout.

The next morning, I arose with a plan. If I left the brownies exposed, I could count on three little boy mice nibbling away until the pan of brownies disappear without a trace. Well, there would be a crumb trail and chocolate splotches on their clothes. Plus, they would be bouncing off the walls with a caffeine and sugar surge.

No, I had to protect the well-being of their teachers and the teen who met the bus and stayed with them until I got home from work. I had to come up with a foolproof way to store the brownies while I was away. Plus, I could not expect the teenage sitter to keep the brownies safe and not indulge in the gooey delight.

So, while the boys were eating breakfast, I pre-heated the

oven. I had lined all the brownie ingredients behind the cereal boxes to avoid detection from inquisitive eyes. I also reminded the boys to make sure they attended to their after-school chores. The oldest boy was responsible for emptying the dishwasher, the middle folded towels, and youngest was supposed to empty the trash.

As soon as the boys were out the door, I whipped up those brownies and put them in the oven while I showered and got ready for work. By the time I was finished making beds, throwing a load of laundry into the dryer, and filling my travel mug with coffee, the brownies were done. I then implemented my plan. I left a note reminding them—again—to do their chores, and off to work I went.

Of course, the telltale smell filled the house. I had hoped that it would dissipate before the munchkins got home. Little did I know, the smell of freshly made brownies would linger all day and haunt three little boys with an olfactory specter.

I arrived home from work, paid the sitter, and walked into the family room. Number 1 son rushed at me and with obvious frustration and self-justified fury he shouted, "Where are they? I can smell them, but I cannot find them. Where did you put them?"

"Whoa, son. I'm happy to see you, too." I replied.

Nonplussed, I asked him if he had done his chores.

He grumbled. "What does that have to do with the brownies?"

"Just asking," I replied while trying to keep the smirk off my face.

Clearly, he was picking up on my non-reaction to his

questions. It only made him more agitated and he uttered a growling sound in exasperation.

"So, then, I can assume that you did not empty the dishwasher as you were supposed to," I countered.

"Mom," he whined, "the smell is driving me crazy. I searched and searched and could not find them."

"Well, why don't you get your scout uniform on, while I cut the brownies for your meeting," I said. "And then we can have our supper," I added.

He stared at me with those chocolate brown eyes, deeper than the brownies he was obsessing about; so bottomless you could only see the pupils in bright daylight. Again, he said, while stretching out each word, "Where . . . are . . . they?"

"Well," I said with more sugar in my voice than was in the brownies, "if you had done your job of emptying the dishwasher, you would have found them cooling on the bottom rack."

With all the dignity he could muster as a ten-year old, he left the room in a huff.

The moral of this story is to remember to do your chores; you never know what kind of wonderful treasure will be in unexpected places.

Epilogue
Fast-forward thirty years, and only several hours after I wrote the above piece. Sometimes, it is startling when a fictionalized version of the truth is truth.

Number 1 son had to evacuate his home on the coast of Florida courtesy of Hurricane Maria. He spent time at his brother's home in the Berkshires and visited family as he meandered south. About 100 miles north of where I live, he phoned that he would make it to my house in time for supper. "Got any brownies, Momma? And milk, too?" he asked with gleeful expectation.

Of course, this mom had brownies made; I knew he was coming and needed all the comforts of home. Will I ever be able to make brownies and not think of him? When he arrives, maybe I should serve them from the dishwasher.

BUSINESS CASUAL
Marie Varley Gillis

After decades as an academic and university-level executive administrator with a high-power, high-stress position, my accomplished husband has accumulated closets full of men's clothing and furnishings. He could outfit a small corporation with impeccably tailored suits that would make any banker or CEO salivate. All the suits are perfectly displayed by color: blue ones, gray ones, black ones, summer stripes, and an extensive collection of sport jackets with coordinating slacks. He has more than fifty dress shirts, starched to extra stiffness; some hang on Mahogany wood hangers, while others are folded and stored in boxes for traveling. As for shoes, well, he has a separate closet dedicated to an impressive collection of Alan Edmonds in every color and style. This is a man who takes dressing very seriously.

However, it is with his ties that he truly demonstrates his sartorial expertise, or perhaps it is a fetish. At last count, they numbered over 250, the majority of which hang on motorized tie racks that rotate with the push of a button. He has been known to squirrel some out of sight in a seldom-used drawer to prevent detection and mocking quips from me. Now, he will claim that he does not own that many, but can a husband ever hide *that* many ties from his wife? He has a rotating system so he does not wear the same tie in any one calendar year. The exception is his favorite Bulgari tie that he saves for very special occasions. He calls it his lucky tie. My dear spouse is also a master of tying the classic

Windsor knot to royal perfection. Oh, and does he have belts. Lots and lots of belts.

However, I think his true GQ personality surfaces when he puts on his hand-tooled Lucchese black cowboy boots. Those beauties, coupled with tight jeans, a big sterling silver buckle belt, and a ten-gallon Stetson pulled low over his brow make this New Englander look like he grew up on a dude ranch. I think he was a Texan in another life.

Now, this introduction is not meant to be a criticism. In fact, it is divine to be on the arm of such a man when he makes an entrance into any venue. However, dear reader, I do want you to have a sense of the background for the rest of my story.

In preparation for the time when we would no longer live in the university-provided house in Georgetown, we purchased a lovely home at the beach, which we nicknamed Sanctuary. It is here that we are now transitioning into sabbatical mode for the next two years. It is a relaxed environment and very casual. He is returning to the research he started while a professor in order to complete the long overdue second edition of one of his books and begin the manuscript of another. Because we outfitted the room over our garage with all the trappings to support his research and writing, his commute and stress levels have been drastically reduced.

Now you have the setting for the first week of moving into Sanctuary...and merging three closets into one jam-packed space.

The first Monday in our new abode, I arose before he, made a pot of coffee, and entered my office. I was just about as content as I can ever remember being; the noises of the city and the demands of our positions were in the rear view mirror.

I was happily typing away and sipping on my coffee when I noticed through peripheral vision that he was standing in my doorway. His body language told me he obviously wanted me to notice something. So, I stopped what I was doing and turned. The spectacle that awaited me was startling.

His hair was so tousled it could not have seen a brush since the day before and his face displayed a two-day stubble (not an attractive look for any man of a certain age, but what looks sort of acceptable on younger men, make him look, well, just scruffy). But it was his attire that truly caught my attention.

He had managed to exhume an ugly green camouflage tee shirt, which was complete with holes and an obvious menu representing spills from past meals. His faded blue gym shorts looked like he sent them to the laundry to be wrinkled. Is it even possible to wrinkle 100% polyester? On his size twelve feet, he was wearing super-furry brown slippers that resembled something the cat had left at the back door.

He accessorized this ensemble with his elegant monogrammed designer brief case that he held in one hand and a travel coffee mug in the other. However, the crowning touch to this vision was the cherished Bulgari tie around his neck, perfectly knotted in a classic Windsor.

With a sparkle in his eyes and a boyish grin, he announced as though I was a member of his staff, "Monday morning and I am ready for work. Hold all calls and take messages. I will be back to take a meeting at noon."

Even he, who has great stage presence, could not

completely keep from giggling or keep his shoulders from shaking ever so slightly before he turned and ascended the staircase to his man cave.

What a vision to behold! I was so stunned that I didn't utter a sound for several seconds. Then, I laughed so heartily that I almost fell off my chair. Tears streamed down my face, and I started to hiccup.

My dear husband had just reinvented the definition of business casual in the telecommuting workplace.

"To reminisce with my old friends, a chance to share some memories, and play our songs again."
— **Ricky Nelson**

Sarah Hardman Giachino was raised in Spencer, West Virginia and is the youngest—and only daughter—of four children. Her father Charles O. Hardman, USA 117th INF 30 DIV, and her mother Mary endured a twenty-month separation during WWll.

All of her life, Sarah listened to her Dad's recollection of his combat experience and understood his deep commitments of sharing his memories with her family and their community. She returned with her parents and family on several trips to the many battlefields and American cemeteries in Europe, retracing his war route while keeping a diary and recording video with photographs.

Early in 2001, Sarah discovered in their family home attic twenty months of consecutive love letters written between her parents and realized the historical importance of their correspondence. In these letters, her father writes to her mother anything unrelated to the danger he faced daily so that she would not worry. He mentions meeting General Eisenhower, crossing the English Channel, liberating villages, sleeping in caves, civilian contacts, helmet baths and more. In these letters, her father also writes of the meaningful visits from the traveling USO Show Troop Vaudeville Performance that lifted the morale of his soldiers in England and France.

Through the discovery of her parents' letters, she has devoted her time to the USO of North Carolina while serving on their Board of Directors. Sarah has published stories in *Chicken Soup for the Veterans Soul* and *Chicken Soup for the Soul, Military Families*. She is currently writing a book titled *Dearest Darling, Dearest Sweetheart,* that will include the letters between her parents. Her book will include firsthand stories from her dad when she toured the battlefields of Europe with him and her mother's memories of struggles in raising their newborn son back home.

Sarah and her husband Nick currently live in Wilmington North Carolina and have two adult daughters, Olivia and Victoria.

BATTLE OF ST. LO, FRANCE
Sarah Hardman Giachino

This story contains a synopsis of the battle courtesy of militaryhistorynow.com, followed by a short collection of letters between my parents.

Battle of St. Lo France—Operation Cobra
July 20–August 8, 1944

Bad weather and a breakdown of communication led to the nastiest blue-on-blue disaster of the entire 1944 Normandy campaign. The incident sprung from an epic 3,000-plane Allied bombing strike aimed at annihilating German defense's near St. Lo, France went awry on July 25. The plan, codenamed Cobra, originally called for British and American planes to drop their payloads as they flew east to west along the length of the enemy lines. Instead, the aircraft came in from the north and unloaded on both the Americans and Germans simultaneously. Low cloud cover prevented the pilots from spotting the friendly forces on the ground. Amazingly, the disaster was a repeat of a similar debacle that occurred only the day before in which 25 Americans were killed. Among the dead on the second day's raid was Lt. Gen. Leslie McNair. He would turn out to be the highest ranking American officer killed in battle in the entire war (ironically a victim of friendly fire). Out of sheer rage, American troops knowingly opened fire on their own planes following the incident.

Thursday, August 3, 1944

I haven't heard from you in a couple of days now and I hope that everything goes well. You wrote that you perhaps would not be able to write for a while so I am expecting this lull—however I hope that it doesn't last too long. Another interesting thing in Nan's letter was that she had heard that the 30th Division was in action on July 24 around Periers and on the Seves river. I don't know where she got that news but I am wondering if it was accurate.

Charles Stanley is 12 weeks old today. I can hardly believe this!

I have made my appt today at the beauty parlor to have my permanent on August 21.

Sleep on it Honey....[lipstick kiss]
I love you sweetheart,
Yo wifie

Friday, August 4, 1944

Dearest Darling,

I received a letter from you yesterday afternoon which I was very happy to see. It was written on the 22nd of July but was postmarked the 27th. I suppose it doesn't go out immediately—and some letters do not get postmarked for several days after they are written....

The news does look real good in the newspapers. I wonder

if you are in on this push to shut-off the Brittany peninsula. Surely this war can't last much longer. I imagine the Germans are doing nothing more than prolonging it now. How I wish you could be home this Oct. 27. This isn't too impossible either is it Darling. I love you so much that every minute away from you makes me long for you more and more.

   Sleep on it Honey……[lipstick kiss]
Yo wifie

Thursday, Aug 3, 1944 [Somewhere in France]

Dearest Darling,

   Honey it's been 2 days since I've had a chance to write and that should be a good indication to you that I've been pretty busy for the last two days…Yes I've been in just a wee bit of combat but here I am just as sound as a dollar and feeling like a million so Darling you should see by that that your ole Hubby knows how to take care of himself. Heck! it isn't as bad as you probably think. Of course Darling this isn't a pleasant task and I for one along with a million or two other soldiers want this to end more than anything else at the moment.

   I <u>really</u> hit the jackpot in the mail last night. I got <u>18</u> letters and 13 of them were from you. I had one swell time reading them and ever sure my morale has been 200% high....

   This afternoon everyone was loaded in trucks and taken to a mobile bathing unit for a good hot shower - Gee but it was wonderful. I think I wrote you about this once before. After we got *back we were issued new clothing from head to toe and now we are entirely different looking bunch of men. Everyone has a shave and haircut and almost look presentable once more. We were also issued these new combat infantry jackets and they are quite stylish. It is a <u>real</u> relief to feel clean once more. We get pretty dirty between baths. I also have a nice roomy fox hole all fixed up with a good sturdy top and my sleeping bag for a bed so I'm all set.... I'll really have a wealth of stories to tell you when I get back. One of the most interesting incidents yet was one day when a battle was going hot & heavy the Germans waved a white flag and stopped things. A Jerry then stepped forward and yelled in English that they would permit our medicals to come into their lines to get American wounded if we would permit them to do the same. Everyone was uncord with the plan so for an hour and a half American & German rubbed elbows while moving their respective wounded. The Germans had taken good care of our boys and bandaged them very well. After everyone was set again the battle started over and was just as hot and heavy as before. It's a heck of a war isn't it? This little incident actually happened.*

    Sweetie, you mentioned the fact that you sometimes get pretty worried about my welfare. I know Sweetie that its almost impassable for you not to be concerned but believe me I'm getting along fine. You are a good soldier and conceal your true feelings.

    ....I've been pretty busy today doing alot of jobs and now I find it is getting almost too dark to write so I'm afraid I'll have to close shortly. I can hardly see what I'm writing now.

    ...so sleep on it, I love you and love you and love you Darling, Sweetest of Dreams and Goodnight Sweetie.
I love you both,

Yo Hubby + Daddy

Sunday, Aug 6, 1944 [V-Mail written in all caps]

DEAREST DARLING,

    I GUESS YOU WILL PROBABLY BE SURPRISED TO BE GETTING V-MAIL# FROM ME BUT I HAD A RATHER UNFORTUNATE INCIDENT AS FAR AS MY STATIONARY WAS CONCERNED. I HAD IT IN MY GAS MASK ALONG WITH MY FLASHLIGHT AND LATEST PICTURES YOU SENT ME OF CHARLES STANLEY AND YOU ALL TAKEN AT SPENCER. I REALLY HATED TO LOSE ALL THOSE PICTURES. THEY WERE REALLY GOOD. SOMEONE TRADED MASKS WITH ME AND NOW ALL I HAVE IS SOMEONE ELSES MASK AND A DISGUSTED FEELING....

    TODAY I HAD A DINNER IN A FRENCH HOUSE. WE HAD BOILED CHICKEN AND POTATOES WITH FRESH BUTTER AND RATHER FUNNY TASTING BREAD. IT WAS PRETTY GOOD UNTIL I HAPPENED TO NOTICE WHAT PART OF THE CHICKEN I WAS EATING. IT WAS THE HEAD, COMB AND ALL —WELL, THAT SORT OF TOOK AWAY MY APPETITE. WE ALSO HAD THE USUAL PORTION OF CIDER WHICH IS USED MORE INSTEAD OF DRINKING WATER. EACH FARM HOUSE HAS TWO OF THESE HUNDRED GALLONS SOME WHERE ABOUT THE HOUSE. I CAN'T SAY THAT I ENJOYED MY FIRST FRENCH MEAL TOO MUCH. MAYBE THE FOOD IN PARIS WILL BE A LITTLE BETTER QUALITY....

    HONEY, I WAS NEVER MORE CONVINCED THAT THERE IS A GOD. HE HAS ANSWERED OUR PRAYERS AND TAKEN VERY GOOD CARE OF ME AND YOU. THERE ARE NO ATHEISTS HERE.

>HONEY, I HOPE YOU WILL BE ABLE TO READ THIS. I PRINTED IT SO I COULD SAY MORE. YOU WILL PROBABLY HAVE TO USE A MAGNIFYING GLASS #
>SLEEP ON IT HONEY...
>I LOVE YOU BOTH
>YO HUBBY + DADDY
>P.S. KISS, KISS, HUG, HUG, KISS, KISS

From the memoirs of Charles O. Hardman as written in 1996 regarding actual events during WWII:

The high command realized that something had to be done to speed our advance to the level area of France where the terrain would be more to our advantage. What followed was the Battle of Saint-Lô.

We were a few miles north of Saint-Lô, a city of about 20,000 and an important road junction. A plan was devised to break out of the hedgerow country by having a concentrated attack by infantry and armor to capture the city. On the morning of July 23rd, we were preparing for this attack, which was supposed to be supported by 3,000 bomber aircraft that were to fly over our heads and bomb the German emplacements. Our troops were withdrawn 1,200 yards from the front to ensure a safety zone between the Germans and us.

The plan was for the planes to see a highway across our front and drop their bombs beyond this point. On paper, this was a good plan, but in reality it was a disaster. The first wave of planes dropped their bombs on us but was stopped by the ground command as soon as the mistake became apparent. Even at that, about twenty-five men from my regiment were killed.

On July 26th the plan was again in force. I was sitting on a hedgerow with a sergeant watching the first wave of planes fly over our heads and bomb the Germans beyond the road as planned. It was a great show as the ground shook like an earthquake, although smoke and soot from that area drifted over the highway and obscured the bomb line. The sergeant said, "Look, Lieutenant, they are dropping them short." I watched with horrible fascination at the planes as I saw black dots coming out of their bomb bays. The dots grew larger and larger until I could hear them whine. I realized they were going to hit us so I dived forward, laid flat on the ground and screamed, *"Please, dear God."* I feel that it was an important instant in my life. I promised that if He would spare me, I would be a better Christian. I was rolled like a log by the blast, but was unhurt.

The entire area had become a disaster. I heard someone calling for help, so I got to my feet and returned to my former hedgerow and found a large crater where I had been sitting. In this crater was one of my men buried up to his chest crying for help and a few feet away was a waving arm sticking out of the ground. I quickly started to dig the soldier's arm out until his head was uncovered and then I worked on the other soldier. My men joined me and we soon had them uncovered.

They were physically unhurt but groggy, so the medics evacuated them. Forty years later, I received a phone call from the soldier whose arm was visible. He said that he had tried since the war to locate me to thank me for saving his life. I was certainly glad to hear from him but I didn't believe I had done anything extraordinary. He located me by seeing my picture in the 30th Division newsletter, a photo that had been taken on one of my trips back to Normandy with my family.

I walked around the area after the bombing and it was a terrible thing to see. In one hedgerow corner about thirty men had sought shelter only to suffer a direct hit by a bomb. There were body parts strewn all around. A truck was loading them to be taken to the rear. I was almost sick at the sight, but that was war, and not uncommon. Altogether, there were around 125 killed and four times that number wounded by the military blunder.

Death and carnage were part of it and I grew calloused to it all except when I lost one of my men. When possible, I made a practice of mailing their personal items to their families with a note of condolence. I usually wrote that they were killed instantly even though that was not always the case. I hoped that would give their loved ones a small comfort to know that they didn't suffer.

As soon as we could round up our men and reform our company, we were part of the main thrust into the German lines. You would have thought that the bombing would have destroyed the enemy, but this was not the case. They arose from their foxholes and bunkers and we had a lively time overcoming them.

My (Sarah's) recollection of living with faithful and God loving parents:

We always attended church every Sunday. As I was

growing up, excuses of oversleeping or just not wanting to go was never tolerated in our home and there was *never* any wiggle room for the slight possibility that I could win that argument. The Sunday morning ritual in our family meant that we left the house at 10:40AM to attend the 11:00 service at St. John's Methodist Church. Our family pew was located on the second row on the far left of the sanctuary.

We were Christians living in the poverty-stricken Bible Belt but I wouldn't consider my parents to be emotional "holy rollers." They both served on church committees and my mother was an avid member of the United Methodist Women.

Daddy said grace every night before dinner by giving thanks for all of their blessings at every meal. I can still hear him say *"Bless the foods to our use and us to our service, keep us ever mindful for the needs of others in your name we ask this. Amen."*

Both of them led by example by always reaching out to those in Appalachia who were less fortunate. Daddy didn't openly display his strong faith by witnessing to others or giving open testimonies in church. That wasn't his style, but he always expressed his thanks and appreciation in others.

On one of our trips overseas, we traveled the same road out from St. Lo along the road to Periers that was the front line between German and American Forces on that bloody morning of July 25, 1944. Until then, I had never heard of the term "friendly fire" and couldn't imagine what it would be like to write a family member of my fallen soldier expressing words of condolences knowing that they had not been killed by the Germans but by an American military blunder.

Daddy recalled that fateful morning as if it had happened

the previous day telling us about his promise to God during the battle when his life was spared. He shared the horrifying details as unreal to him today and compared to the wonderful what he had lived since then—a successful business and steady day-to-day living in a small wonderful town with his wife, children, and grandchildren.

Up until that moment, I had never seen my dad cry. But he was crying then as he concluded, "I have thanked God every single day of my life for the privilege of being an American."

And I knew he meant it, too.

I'M THE ONE YOU'VE BEEN LOOKING FOR
Sarah Hardman Giachino

During the height of the Vietnam War, my country was struggling with political dissention and patriotism was on trial. Many citizens were questioning why the United States was involved in this misunderstood war and demonstrated their anger in a public forum by insulting many returning service members who were deployed for several months in South Vietnam.

In 1970, I was fourteen years old and a freshman at Spencer High School in rural Spencer, West Virginia. My dad served in WWll and paying respect to our country was always honored in our family. As the daughter of a veteran, I couldn't understand the student outcry of disgust that I saw on television showing public displays of anger using destructive tactics like flag burning and rioting in major cities such as Detroit, Chicago, and Washington, DC.

"A-walling" to Canada was not an option for my two older brothers who were commissioned and currently serving in the Army. They quite possibly could be deployed, too, but my dad made it clear in our home, *"If you are called to serve, you serve. Period."*

I learned through a close friend that Prisoner of War (POW) bracelets were available and could be worn to show support for our service members who were being held captive in Vietnam. Each nickel plated or copper bracelet was etched with name, rank and the date of capture and cost $2.50-3.00.

I wanted one.

Weeks later, I received in the mail a small packet from an unknown address that contained the copper bracelet with the inscription "Robert W. Barnett, Lt Col Air Force, Oct 3, 1967."

Robert was now my POW. I began to feel personally connected to this war and wore his bracelet every single day for the next twenty-five months, bearing the responsibility to show honor and respect for him. Robert accompanied me to my first high school homecoming, twirling a baton of fire at our High School halftime football games, New Year's Eve ski trips at Snowshoe, West Virginia, and August vacations at Wrightsville Beach, North Carolina.

Robert never left my side and I never removed his bracelet. In class, my mind would wander and I would often study his name etched on my bracelet and wonder what he was doing at the moment. Was he hurt? Was he denied food and water? Did they torture him every day? Was he even alive?

Our family always watched the *Evening News with Walter Cronkite* every night after dinner at 6:30 and each night, the news about Vietnam was increasingly dismal. CBS started to show flag draped coffins returning from Vietnam and I wondered if Robert might be in one of those.

One evening, Cronkite announced that the POWs were going to be released and his broadcast would cover their return home. For the next few evening broadcasts, I kept my eyes peeled on the portable black and white TV sitting on our kitchen counter in hopes that I would see his name announced and printed on the bottom of the screen as he walked down the steps of the plane at the Air Force Base in California.

Finally, on one evening news edition of March 1973, I spied LT COL Robert W. Barnett's name flash at the bottom of the screen. "Look, Mother and Daddy, it's him!" I exclaimed.

We all froze and watched his brief appearance on television as he descended the steps from the plane and disappeared behind the reporter as the next newly released hero appeared.

I was thrilled beyond words. My hero was home! Now what? I understood through the POW bracelet program that a tiny little white star on a blue sticker was available to stick on the bracelet if your POW was released and arrived stateside, so I ordered one and proudly attached it to my bracelet.

Many years passed and eventually Robert found his way to the bottom of my jewelry box. Through four years of college, job relocations, marriage, two babies and all the moves that accompanied these stages of my life, Robert traveled with me. I held on to the bracelet because this part of my life honoring Robert had special meaning. It was a reminder that in some strange way, maybe I had a small part in bringing him home by never ever giving up hope that he would return to his family.

In 2008, we were living in St. Charles, Illinois and on one cold February day, I decided to clean out my jewelry box. There he was, buried underneath an antique sterling silver bracelet and several plastic bangles. I had not taken a really good look at my tarnished copper POW bracelet in decades, so I took a moment to study it closely.

What if he is still alive? I wondered. *What if I could find him on the Internet?*

Immediately, I dropped what I was doing, sat down to my computer and typed "ROBERT W. BARNETT VIETNAM POW." Right away, a biography appeared under the name of BARNETT, ROBERT WARREN compiled by P.O.W. NETWORK from a source called WE CAME HOME copyright 1977.

His biography read, "*As I write this on 3 April 1973, I'm at my parent's house in Medicine Hat, Alberta, Canada. I was released from Hanoi 14 March and arrived at March AFB, California on the 17th where I met my wife, Anita; daughter, Lori: my sister Doreen: my brother Don; His family and many other friends. I was finally home.*"
It went on to describe his life as a pilot and the unfortunate circumstances of his capture and life in the "Hanoi Hilton" for 1,989 days.

His biography also mentioned that he was retired from the United States Air Force as a Colonel and he and his wife, Anita lived in Arizona. I was ecstatic beyond words!

Right away, I began to type in a search for a Robert W. Barnett in Arizona and one appeared on the screen with a phone number in Tucson. Immediately, I picked up the phone and dialed the number on my screen, not knowing what in the world I was going to say to anybody that might answer. As luck would have it, a voice message answered asking me to leave my name, number and a brief message.

"Hi, uhh, this is Sarah Giachino calling you from St, Charles IL. I am hoping that I have reached the correct Lt Col Robert W. Barnett that served in Vietnam and was captured and spent years as a POW. The reason I am calling is that when I was fourteen years old, I wore a copper POW bracelet with your name on it and I am hopeful that this is you. Call me at 555.555.5555. I would like for you to know how grateful I am to you and would like to return my bracelet to you. Goodbye."

I really had no clue if I was ever going to hear from anybody on the other end and decided to dismiss the thought that Robert or a family member would return a random phone message like mine. I really didn't know for sure if I reached the correct Robert W. Barnett. After all, it had been thirty-eight years since I slipped his bracelet on my wrist and after enduring years as prisoner of war in North Vietnam, he could be in ill health and maybe not alive. At least I was certain he returned home to his wife and I was satisfied knowing this.

Three months later, I was in our library when I heard the phone ring in the kitchen and my husband Nick answered. After a brief moment I heard him cautiously say, "May I ask *who* is calling Sarah?" We had been receiving many telemarketing calls and I sensed he was about to hang up when I heard him say, "Bob? Bob who? Barnett? Uh, I don't think she..."

I jumped out of my chair and ran into the kitchen and grabbed the phone out of his hand. With great excitement, I calmly and slowly said, "This is Sarah..."

Meanwhile, Nick stood there with his arm still raised as if he were still holding the phone, staring at me confused and completely dumbfounded. I could read his lips as he silently mouthed, "Who is this?" while at the same time I heard a voice on the receiver say, "This is Bob Barnett, I am the one you have been looking for."

Quite honestly, I am not sure what I said to him immediately after that. I was filled with so much joy that I am certain I reverted to a giddy teenager who had just received a phone call from an admirer. But I do remember telling him that I saw him exit the plane on the *Evening News with Walter Cronkite* and was relieved that he made it home.

He recalled that day because when he reached the bottom step from the plane, he saw a journalist approach him and then bypassed him to talk to somebody else. He said that was his first impression of returning home. I also asked him if he knew that his name was on a POW bracelet and he said his sister had told him there were several bracelets inscribed with his name.

I offered to return my bracelet to him and asked for his address. But instead, he asked me to keep his bracelet and thanked me for thinking of him every single day while he was in captivity.

We exchanged Christmas cards for many years, and he always wrote on the back of the cards how much he appreciated my current support of today's military.

If anybody thinks that thoughts and prayers for our Missing in Action and our Prisoners of War are not effective, then I beg to differ. I was just a fourteen-year-old small-town girl who *never gave up.*

"No memory is ever alone; it's at the end of a trail of memories, a dozen trails that each have their own associations."
— **Louis L'Amour**

Diane Torgersen was born in Brooklyn, New York and has lived many places in the States. She, her husband, and three sons lived in Texas and Alaska before finally settling down in Maryland. She later spent three years in Cheltenham, England, where she attended the Gloucestershire College of Art and Design.

Diane remarried and continued studying and working in art and design. They moved to Florida where she began designing art pillows, becoming known as The Pillow Lady of the East Coast. She then moved to Wilmington, North Carolina where she studied abstract painting at UNCW.

Diane has aspired to be a writer since writing essays in the third grade, two of which she still possesses. She has always had a thread of writing throughout her life while pursuing other interests and careers. Her "official" entry into the writing world began when she joined the Landfall Writers' Group in Wilmington in 2015 where she found a strong voice writing reflective humor. These stories are mostly drawn from childhood, observations, raising a family, and simply living—all done with a commitment to preserving those cherished memories.

CHEATING AND REDEMPTION
Diane Torgersen

I was in the third grade before I really understood the value of—or punishment for—trying to cheat at something. I'm sure I had attempted or even was successful at doing something in an inappropriate way before, but this was the first time I remember being caught at it.

We were trying to learn the multiplication tables in school and I was having an awful time with them. I just couldn't get past the "times fives." My dad worked with me each night, but it just wasn't sticking in my memory. I seemed to have no facility for translating those numbers into something I could remember or memorize. I remember feeling desperate and not wanting the shame of failing the test.

I came to school knowing that I did not know the tables past the fives and sat staring at the paper when I could go no further. I peeked at the desks around me. We kids at that age wrote in big letters. I could see some of my fellow student's papers!

I kept looking around, trying to fill out some of the areas on my test by copying theirs. When the teacher caught me at it and called my name from across the room, it felt like the air had left my body. I was mortified that she would bring attention to me like that.

She asked me to bring her my paper and to stay after school. I sat thru the rest of the test with an empty desk surface before me.

At the end of the day, she explained to me what "cheating" was. I had nothing to offer for my behavior other than I simply did not know the tables past the fives. They just didn't make sense to me. I could see the rhythm and sequence of them, but I couldn't retain them. She told me that I would not go on to the fourth grade if I did not learn them. From that point on, I only remember the tears dripping down on my hands and simply wanting out of that room. I could win spelling bees, but I could not do math.

Somehow, I managed to memorize them long enough to pass the test and went on to the fourth grade. That year, the class beauty sat in front of me, allowing me to admire and remember her perfect outfits each day. Very illuminating and intimidating. Fortunately for me, the others around me were the class clowns. I could relate to them more easily: cute little guys and always ready to devastate with a look or whispered commentary.

On one particular test day, one of the class clowns—in the midst of the test, when the teacher had left the room—laid four one-dollar bills across the top of his desk and asked for the answer to a particular question.

Why this one question was that important to him, I will never know, but his standing among us changed that day. We couldn't look at him and ignored his whispered question. I understood his desperation, having been there myself, but I was embarrassed for him, too. When the teacher returned, he picked up the four bills and put them back into his wallet.

I still see him at reunions and this is the image I have

retained of him. However, there is redemption: He has been a principal of a high school in his teaching career.

There has been redemption for me, too: The invention of calculators, since I *still* don't know the multiplication tables above the "times fives."

MY MEDICAL CAREER
Diane Torgersen

I think I was about eight years old when I did my first "touch-less" suturing job. My parents had left me in charge, babysitting my two-year-old brother and five-year-old sister. My brother somehow had cut the end of one of his toes off and hopped to me with it dangling by a tiny piece of skin.

I thought I was going to be in Big Trouble if I didn't come up with a remedy. I got him into the bathroom, cleaned him up and put a big piece of tape around it. That seemed to work well. My brother stopped wailing and was stumping around, admiring his white toe.

I told my parents that he had hurt his toe, hence the tape. I guess they just kept changing the bandage because I don't remember them saying anything. To this day, my brother still shows me the little bump on the end of one of his toes.

Another time of babysitting (same ages), my sister was running with a popsicle stick in her mouth. She came running to me with this thing sticking in the roof of her mouth! I yanked it out and got her something to drink. She seemed to be okay, so I didn't mention this outpatient procedure to my parents. It was so odd.

Years later, she was telling me about not being able to have some specific dental work done "due to a large lump on the roof of her mouth." It was then that I thought to tell her what I had done that day. She had just been assuming that all people had lumps there. I must have done a good job since no dentist ever told her, either. Did I mention she had a beautiful voice and sang in nightclubs for a time? Surely my medical expertise had something to do with that.

Around this same year, one of our aunts was visiting. And, as usual, my parents were gone when a medical emergency came up. She accidentally stuck her fingers into an oscillating fan and cut two or three of them. Back into the bathroom for the roll of tape. I can still see my aunt with her three bandaged fingers sticking out. I tended to use quite a bit of tape and gauze back then, and my parents were becoming very proud of my work.

Then there was my dad. He was forever whacking or cutting himself with something, being a do-it-himselfer. Once the head of a pickax came off while he was digging something outside and it hit his head. Mom called me to come help. This truly needed stitching and I definitely wasn't up to that part of my medical experience yet as this was beyond tape and gauze. I did drive him (despite being only fourteen) to the only doctor in town who took care of it.

That winter, a kerosene heater in the house exploded and he saved us by carrying it outside. He had terrible third-degree burns on that side of his body. I again drove him to the doctor.

Since it was a Sunday, the doctor did not want to spend time cleaning the petroleum product off his skin. He told me to take him back home and wash the burned areas.

I demanded that he at least give my dad something for shock because even at that age, I could see that he was not doing well. No hope for it. I have seldom in my life been as physically angry at someone as I was that day.

I took dad back home and mother and I gently washed those areas, then back to the doctor's office on Monday, where he finally took care of dad. Over the years, I would occasionally run into that doctor and all I could think to do was stand and stare him down, knowing he knew exactly what I was remembering.

As a parent, I have handled minor emergencies with my children such as skinned knees, broken arms and teeth knocked loose by bike falls. Fortunately, there weren't too many of those. I don't know whether they became more careful or I became more wily in preventive care. In any case, I can still do a mean bandage.

CREATIVE AWARENESS
Diane Torgersen

My first literary success was plagiarizing Edgar Allen Poe in the fourth grade. We were to write a story and create a cover for it. I titled it *The Storm*. To increase my star quality, I had covered thick paper with a shiny emerald green aluminum-like wrapping paper and stapled the two sheets front and back to my purloined story. It was gaudy, but impressive. Apparently, my teacher had not read Edgar Allen Poe since she wrote a very nice note on my work saying that I was a good writer and she liked what I had done.

Later that summer I wrote 100 short stories on 100 sheets of notebook paper. I remember that some of them were no longer than a paragraph. I must have pestered my mother to read them, showing them to her over and over. I wanted acclaim for what I had created, and she was the nearest victim of my fame-driven attitude. I don't remember what she said, but I do remember that Look.

Mother had a Damon Runyan, *Guys and Dolls* vernacular sometimes and the Look said, "Go away, Bud—you bother me." So, I took them outside, piled up small sticks, struck a match and burned them. A funeral pyre to my unappreciated literary masterpieces.

That same year, I wanted to be part of a local talent show to be held on the stage of the elementary school, which was open to the public. The only talent I thought I had was a xylophone given to me for some birthday or Christmas event. It had a small number of keys, but I thought what I played sounded good enough to win one of the prizes that were being offered.

I have no idea how I got my parents to agree to take me there, but I do remember sitting on the piano bench someone had kindly moved center stage, propping my instrument on my lap, and beginning to tap away with two little hammers.

Then I made the mistake of looking at the audience and seeing nothing but faces. My legs started to shake, and this seemed to enhance my performance because the audience began to cheer and clap and keep time while my legs bounced up and down.

I always wondered if they thought I was really getting into the rhythm and joy of what I was creating on the spot, or if they were just kind and trying to help me escape with dignity.

One of my favorite facts of life has always been that sometimes you do things simply because you didn't know you couldn't do them. My parents enrolled me in a piano class after that.

CRITIQUES
Diane Torgersen

It might be hard to be a critic—one who reviews books or art—but I think it is often harder to be on the receiving end, to feel like a victim or feel the loss of your own aspirations and enthusiasms. Where do the lines of integrity fall? Do they reject work for fun, a salary or for their own promotion?

There are many who relish negative commentary and the rowdy criticisms that sell more papers or magazines; those who promote their reputations for their own enjoyment. But I also know there are sincere critics as well. I've met them over the years and have been fortunate enough to have had personal experiences and critiques by them. They are the nurturing ones, who seem able to tell their own truth but do no harm.

I remember one art show for which I worked hard to finish pieces to be considered for the juried entry. I had been an artist for many years, but I had not participated in entries for a number of those years. I had recently changed my painting style and was wanting confirmation for the reality of having done that. Entrants were to submit only one piece for the jurors to consider for hanging and judging. Mine was not selected.

We had been directed to pick up our rejects at specific times. I had brought plastic to cover my work since it was raining. I was taping it shut and was preparing to carry it out to the car when a woman walked up to me. I recognized her as one of the executive art directors for the facility. One whose opinion I had always valued and never missed any commentaries she would do.

She bent down and began un-taping my abstract canvas while saying, "This one should have made it into the exhibit." And she began to tell me what she saw in my piece: the colors and lines used in the abstract, the semi-forms that created suggestions and ideas within the painted surfaces. I would rather have had those few minutes with her personal critique than any chance of having my artwork hung in the exhibit. Her encouragement is memorable, even to this moment.

Another odd critique I remember was after we had moved to Florida. I joined the local artists group and signed up to submit some of my work for the next local artist's show. I took three of my best pieces and left them for consideration for entry into the juried show. I was later notified to return to pick up the pieces that hadn't been accepted. Much to my surprise, all three were returned. One of them had won an award in Maryland; these really were some of my best works to date.

I could hardly wait to go to the opening of the show to see what my competition was. It didn't take long to determine the problem: every single painting being shown was in Florida pastel colors: pinks, yellow, blue, aqua, light greens! Mine were the darker, "northern" colors.

I did learn to paint in these light-hearted colors. One of the canvases I painted for another exhibit was chosen to be part of a six-month tour around the States, featuring Florida work.

HOME IS WHERE DIFFERENT IS
Diane Torgersen

I learned that home is where different is...and that different can be a growing experience. A chance to make choices, have opinions.

Such as mother changing the kitchen colors so often that we had opportunities to make decisions about styles, tints, complementary colors, Winters, Springs. Once it was orange and pink. This created a soft glow as long as you didn't mind very warm colors. I remember that the pink was soft, but I thought it all worked very well with the appliances and stainless-steel sinks. See what I mean? You begin to make comparisons, even at a young age.

Another year the kitchen was green and blue. Triadic colors, split complementary colors, some next to each other on the color wheel. I'm not even sure mother told us that. It was such a violent combination that we knew it had to have an important name. Think crashing sea waves and deep pine forests.

Linens were always an issue. They usually had stiff oil paint stains on them since mother was not above using items from the linen closet to clean her artist brushes. I finally decided to always have a set hidden away, so I could set them out in the bathroom when we had guests. She was fortunate to have had two girls first and that one of them was a Martha Stewart prototype. "Keep moving, or she will clean you" she would sometimes say.

Mom was a Bohemian flower child before there was such a thing. She possessed a graceful attitude toward all living creatures. Her greatest moments involved joy, fun, and laughter, but she was always available for serious, sit-down talks about the complexities of life.

I finally exited my adventurous food-seeking childhood and became Joan of Arc, Wonder Woman and a secret Max Factor experimenter. I was allowed to cook anything that I liked since Mother's interest in food reflected what day of the week it was. Friday: chili and macaroni; Sunday: chicken and potato salad. I always liked her cooking, though. Since she was handicapped and had only one hand to use, she didn't spend much time stirring and mashing, so we learned to love the lumps in food. Somehow, it's strangely comforting even now.

She made the most memorable fudge. My dad craved it. One evening, we had had liver and onions for dinner and he ate a huge meal followed by a huge piece of her fudge. He returned to the kitchen later and was going to have another piece, but she said "no." So, he settled for a liver sandwich.

He headed back to his chair in the living room holding his sandwich, with a wicked smile of satisfaction on his face. He winked at us, lifted one side of the bread, and showed us a generous hunk of fudge nestled under the liver.

Childhood can indeed be a delicious teaching ground.

"Life is not a problem to be solved, but a reality to be experienced."
— **Soren Kierkegaard**

Doris Chew was born and raised in Lower Manhattan in New York City. Her parents emigrated from China to the United States in the 1930s and 1950s. She attended Stuyvesant High School, SUNY at Stony Brook and New York University School of Law. She went on to practice law in Manhattan for twenty-five years, including at a prestigious Wall Street law firm and a major insurance company.

She and her husband, Bill Stewart, recently moved from Ridgewood, New Jersey to Wilmington, North Carolina. They have two beautiful daughters, Avery and Lindsay (ages 23 and 21 respectively), who were adopted from China and New York. Her daughters' Chinese names, when translated into English, mean "Beautiful Star" - one from the East and one from the West.

Doris is currently writing a memoir to show her daughters that life is a journey that has many different paths. She hopes to inspire her daughters to follow the call of their hearts and take those different - sometimes winding - paths to their destiny.

A CONVERSATION ABOUT DEATH AND DYING
Doris Chew

Except for one uncle, I grew up without any extended family in the United States. My mother and my uncle were the only two of five siblings to emigrate here. My father emigrated to the U.S. alone as a teenager. Since we didn't have any grandparents or other close relatives here, the conversation about death and dying never came up for most of my adult life. In one day, that all changed.

On September 10, 2001, my father-in-law, Archie, who I knew for twenty years, passed away after battling eye cancer for one year. He was only seventy years old.

During his illness, I didn't visit him because of my hectic schedule at work and my daughters' jam-packed activities. Since I didn't know anyone who had died of cancer, it never occurred to me that he might not recover.

Archie was a tough-talking, no-nonsense commanding officer in the Army who instilled fear in his subordinates, but secretly had a heart of pure gold. I felt fortunate that he shared his heart with me in the many hours we spent together. We talked about the homeless problem in New York City, the best bourbons, growing up in the South and life in the Army, but we never had a conversation about death and dying.   Archie was the first person I knew and loved that passed away. I hoped that attending his funeral would help me accept his death.

On September 11, 2001, my daughters were scheduled to

fly first to Ohio with their dad and then I planned on traveling there a few days later for the funeral. Since it was a school day, the girls were to be taken out of the classroom to meet their dad at the principal's office at noon.

That morning, like a typical overachieving parent, I insisted that my six-year-old daughter spell all the words correctly for me as a review for the spelling test she was taking later that day in her first-grade class. Because my daughter struggled with the practice spelling test, it took longer than I expected.

I was annoyed that I missed my usual train and caught the 8:05AM train instead, which was due to arrive at 8:50AM at Hoboken, New Jersey. As the train rolled slowly into the station, I saw thick black smoke ferociously pouring through a gaping hole at the top of the World Trade Center North tower. Despite the ominous backdrop of the billowing black smoke, I still remember the rational, and not yet fearful, conversation I had with myself that day.

Why is there black smoke billowing out of the World Trade Center? There must have been a plane accident. The Path train underneath the World Trade Center will be delayed, so it would be a smart plan to take the ferry across the Hudson River, instead.

As I waited for the ferry at the pier, the image of the looming chimney stacks spouting black smoke against the clear blue sky became increasingly unsettling, so I took out my compact Canon camera that I always carried in my handbag to capture candid moments of my daughters. Through the lens of the camera, I suddenly saw another plane appear from behind the burning North tower and watched it crash into the South tower!

Instantly, the casual chatter of the commuters stopped as everyone held their collective breath in shock and then, almost in unison, said those scary words out loud: "It's a terrorist attack!" Then it was cacophony as frantic commuters yelled into their cell phones and to each other and emergency instructions blared from the intercoms.

In contrast to the chaotic commotion on the pier, I remembered the utter silence on the train when the first ferry boat of passengers arrived from the New York side of the Hudson River. The passengers, with ashen skin and blank stares, slowly and wordlessly filed past us on the train. The stunned silence on the forty-five-minute train ride was only punctuated by one of the passengers, who had a portable transistor radio that was announcing the latest terrifying events: a plane has hit the Pentagon, a plane has crashed in Pennsylvania, the U.S. airspace is closed, bridges and tunnels to New York City are closed, the South tower collapsed and then the North tower.

While on that train, I suddenly felt a desperate need to get home and hold my two precious daughters close to me as the randomness of who was able to go home that day shook me to my core.

I often think about how close I came to dying that day in September. For twenty years, I commuted into the World Trade Center at that exact time the first plane hit the North tower. I would have been on the Path train underneath the towers or walking on the concourse lobby or just exiting the buildings.

For months, I had terrifying nightmares of chards of glass and blocks of concrete raining down on the pedestrians emerging from the World Trade Center; of the plummeting elevator of fire ferociously barreling out the concourse lobby and engulfing commuters in its path as the vacuum of air sucked the balls of fire out the doors and into the streets; of the concrete and steel collapsing on the Path train and trapping the commuters underneath the buildings.

It is scary, and sobering, when I think about my random luck of not being one of the victims that day. Because I was late for work, I was spared while many others perished. For forty-seven years, I didn't think about death and dying but now, not only is it a normal part of my conversation, it is also a permanent part of the national consciousness.

I never made it to my father-in-law's funeral. As with the many relatives of victims that died on 9/11, it was upsetting to me that I didn't get a chance to pay my final respects and say good-bye to Archie.

However, I now believe that our relationship will not judged on whether I was there on the day he died, but whether I was there in his life when he was alive. If I had that conversation about death and dying with Archie, I think he would tell me to counter the randomness of death by always being there for each other in life.

In the end, that's all that matters.

LESSONS FROM NUMBER 2 DAUGHTER
Doris Chew

My life has been a series of chosen paths at crossroads which lead to new experiences. My philosophy is best summed up by Ralph Waldo Emerson when he said, "Do not go where the path may lead. Go instead where there is no path and leave a trail...."

Identity

I grew up in a government housing project near New York City's Chinatown. I had an older sister, one brother and a younger sister. I am the middle sister; the Number 2 Daughter.

In a Chinese family, the Number 2 Daughter has no status in the family. When I was six or seven years old, a family friend came to visit us from Hong Kong. After dinner, the Chinese custom is for the visitor to present gifts to the family.

The family friend handed out a beautiful gold heart necklace to the oldest daughter, another lovely gold necklace with a small cross to the youngest daughter and finally, a thick, gold chain with a piece of apple green jade to the only son. I waited for my gift, but the family friend forgot to bring one for the middle daughter!

As I stood there with my siblings, I remembered feeling invisible and embarrassed to be the Number 2 Daughter. It was at that moment that I resolved to create my own identity. I wasn't pretty enough to be the "pretty one." I didn't play any sports, so I couldn't be the "athletic one," and I certainly couldn't pretend to be the "funny one." I decided, however, that I could study hard enough to become the "smart one" in the family.

And I did. I got into the gifted Special Program class in junior high school, tested into an exclusive math and science high school (in only the second class after the school admitted girls), lived on the college campus against my mother's wishes, and finally, was admitted to a prestigious law school as only one of six Asians out of a class of 350 students.

For many years, my mother would proudly introduce her kids to family and friends as her only son, oldest daughter, youngest daughter, and the smart daughter!

The lesson here is that you can decide to be whomever you want to be and then work hard to become that person. You *can* shape your own destiny!

Work

My first job out of law school was as an in-house lawyer for an insurance policy and rating company. It was not my dream job. After six years, I realized it was a mistake not to work at a major law firm in order to build a foundation for my legal career.

Even though working as an in-house corporate lawyer was my ultimate goal, I never had a mentor to advise me of the desirable building blocks that the legal profession required to achieve your ultimate dream job. Unbelievably, I interviewed and was hired to help start an insurance practice at the third largest law firm in the world!

Fortunately for me, insurance corporate practice was a new emerging field and the law firm was desperate to find associates to service some existing insurance clients. It was a crazy and stressful time that required working late nights and weekends, but it was also a heady time to be surrounded by some of the best and brightest lawyers in the country!

After a few years, this law firm imploded by its strategy of acquisition by growth and filed for bankruptcy. Our entire insurance practice moved to another smaller "white-shoe" law firm on Wall Street. In those days, a "white-shoe" firm was considered a stodgy, old, East Coast firm run by members of the WASP elite.

This 100-year-old firm of 100 lawyers didn't have any women partners and only two female associates, including me! At this firm, I caught a fascinating glimpse through a tiny window of how the upper 1 percent of the elite lived and worked. After working there for six years, I finally was able to get my dream job working as in-house counsel for a large prestigious insurance company in Manhattan.

The lesson here is to always try something new and don't be afraid to fail. Even if you fail, you will learn something new. For me, it certainly helped that I didn't fully appreciate how gigantic some of the obstacles were. Otherwise, I might have been more afraid to fail!

Family

My ex-husband and I tried for ten years to start a family. We went to numerous fertility doctors and endured painful treatments and surgical procedures, but nothing worked.

One summer day in 1992, I happened to hear on the *Sally Rafael* talk show about a family that just adopted a baby girl from China through the Pearl S. Buck Foundation in Pennsylvania. A light bulb instantly went off in my head!

Although we were warned of the political and legal uncertainties surrounding this new China adoption program, we immediately submitted an adoption application in 1992. The application required a mountain of documents that needed to be separately certified, notarized and authenticated by the local, county, state and federal governments and all translated into Mandarin Chinese.

It was a long and often frustrating process, complete with a moratorium on all China adoptions as we waited for China to draft regulations in compliance with the Hague Treaty for international adoptions. We also had to endure a change in adoption agencies due to our original agency's lack of personnel within China to assist with the adoption process.

Although the obstacles seemed overwhelming, I was determined not to give up. I wrote the U.S. State Department to enlist their assistance in the adoption process and had the adoption agency's phone number on speed dial to get the latest updates on our file as it slowly traveled from one government agency to the next for review and approval.

Finally, in 1994, we were approved and received one tiny 2"x2" photo of our new daughter who was maybe one-month old in the picture with no background information. For the next six months, we helplessly stared at our daughter in this tiny photo and hoped that she was being well cared for as we waited for our adoption group to be approved to travel to Anhui Province, China, a poor industrial city.

In June, 1994, I held our daughter, Avery, who was then six-and-a-half months old and weighed only thirteen-and-a-half pounds, for the first time in a hotel room in China. At that moment, a deep sense of happiness, gratitude and relief overwhelmed me to the point that I had to sit down in order to hold her!

I later found out that China first allowed adoptions to the United States in 1991 and only sixty-one children were issued immigrant visas. Avery was one of 787 Chinese adoptions in the U.S. that year. Since then, there have been more than 90,000 Chinese adoptions in the U.S.

Two years later, we adopted our second daughter, Lindsay. Unlike Avery, she was a domestic baby from Long Island. We had just completed an application at the adoption agency for a second baby from China when the adoption agency called and left an urgent message.

A young Chinese woman had walked into the office and wanted to find parents for her soon-to-be born baby. In a flurry of activity, we, together with several other prospective families, submitted our application and profile the same day. To our great surprise and shock, we were chosen to be the lucky parents!

Unexpectedly, the baby was born the very next day. One week later, we were holding a precious and beautiful infant girl, our second daughter, Lindsay. Unlike Avery's two-year adoption ordeal, Lindsay's adoption took only ten days!

The lesson here is to pursue your dreams and never, ever give up on achieving them! My life dream, above all else, was to be a mother. Although the path was long, winding and often filled with potholes, I was determined to stay on that path until it finally lead me to my two precious daughters!

My words cannot adequately describe how much they mean to me, but that feeling of overwhelming happiness and gratitude when they first arrived in my life will always be with me.

OCEAN'S EDGE
Doris Chew

I stand on the sand as the heavy sun sets over Ocean.

I watch Ocean, mesmerized by the constant rolling waves of her body.

I listen to Ocean, lulled by the soft rumblings of her soul.

Slowly, I am pulled to Ocean's edge and feel her cool waves tickle my toes.

Feel the joy in riding Ocean's waves, the highs and lows and ins and outs. Wade deeper and immerse yourself in the sea change. The water is shimmering with the golden light of the setting sun.

Come in, don't be afraid. Discover Ocean's wonders in its deeps.

This will be your best Life.

"Stories have inspired me all my life. I like reading about what other people have done and it inspires me to share my own stories, and encourage people to make their own life stories."
— **Phil Keoghan**

John Roper was born in Boston, Massachusetts and lived in Massachusetts, New York, Delaware, Pennsylvania, and California before spending the majority of his adult life in Connecticut.

He received his undergraduate degree at West Chester University, earned a Master's degree in world history at the University of Bridgeport, as well as thirty credits at California State University at Fresno in radio, television and film, and thirty credits at Fairfield University in educational computing.

He taught in the Fairfield Public School system for thirty-nine years and coached boys' and girls' cross country, indoor and outdoor track. In 1981, he was awarded a summer fellowship at Yale University and researched and coauthored *Curriculum Units on Connecticut History* (Yale University Press, New Haven, 1981).

In 2007, he and his wife retired to Wilmington North Carolina. He has two sons: one of whom lives in Chicago, and the other in New Jersey. He has done volunteer work for the University of North Carolina at Wilmington track team, the Cameron Museum, local road races, and a yoga studio.

He began writing in 2014 as therapy following the death of his wife and enjoys the support, camaraderie, and constructive suggestions of the Landfall Writers' Group.

A MEDICAL MIRACLE
John Roper

"Damn! I did it again!" I said holding my forehead.

Amy stared at me. She didn't have to say a word; I knew exactly what she was thinking.

I told you it was a mistake to buy this house.

But, I was taken by it. I had had enough of living in the city—the dirt, the noise, the congestion. So when we saw this colonial for sale in Southport, Connecticut, I fell in love.

It was built by a former sea captain who retired after a prosperous career. The house at one time had been magnificent, but over the years had fallen into disrepair.

I saw the romance of restoring it to its former glory. Amy saw it as a money pit.

We talked over many plans to renovate the kitchen and the bathrooms, watched HGTV religiously every night, and created a large file of clippings from home design magazines. But, everything was in the planning stage. I could visualize how the house would be a marvelous blend of new efficiency and historic charm. Amy, however, just wanted our apartment in the city.

I had only one problem with the house. I was 6'3" whereas Captain Blair had been 5'8". The doorways reflected his height, and I kept banging my head whenever I forgot to duck going through them. I did not to complain to Amy as I didn't want to give her any ammunition to use against the house. So that morning, I simply grabbed some ice, put it in a plastic bag, and iced my aching head on the way to the train station.

The commute into the city took about one hour and fifteen minutes, something I used as an argument for buying the house. "The commute will give me an extra two-and-a-half hours each day to get work done. I can work on my phone or laptop as I commute. By the time I get home, I should be caught up on everything, and we can just have some wine, eat, and relax," I said to convince my skeptical wife.

I was also fascinated by the history of the house. When Captain Blair built it in 1815, Andrew Jackson was fighting the battle of New Orleans, Napoleon was defeated at Waterloo, and James Madison was president. Generations had been born, grew up, married, lived, and died in the house, and the prospect of researching the people who lived there sparked my imagination.

I loved the high ceilings, the crown molding, the plaster medallions that anchored exquisite chandeliers. She had once been a spectacular beauty, and I wanted to restore her to her former glory.

Amy saw only dirt, cobwebs, rust, and cracked plaster.

We were young and energetic and I was filled with optimism that we could make this house a showplace. I had excellent health except for one thing: I was having a problem with headaches. They would come out of nowhere, last a few minutes to hours, and magically disappear.

My job in finance required long hours at work, and I didn't want to take any time off. However, Beth, one of my coworkers recommended an online concierge doctor. I Googled her recommendation, paid with my credit card and a short time later, a very professional looking Doctor Gosh appeared on Skype.

After describing my symptoms, he recommended that I find some time to relax when I get home, do moderate exercise, meditate, try yoga, and take ibuprofen when I felt pain.

He seemed to know what he was talking about, so I thanked him and followed his advice. Amy looked at me suspiciously when I told her I wanted to do yoga, but we enjoyed taking a class together at the "Y" on Thursday nights.

Although ibuprofen alleviated the headaches, they kept coming back. So, I Skyped Doctor Gosh again and he referred me to Doctor Emily Wu, a neurologist.

"Are you claustrophobic?" asked Doctor Wu, clad in her white lab coat, most likely to give her more credibility since she appeared to be about seventeen years old.

"No, why?"

"Because I'm ordering an MRI and some people have a hard time being in the machine's confined space for about forty-five minutes."

"I think I'll be okay," I replied.

"I'm going to prescribe an anti-anxiety medication that I want you to take about thirty to sixty minutes before the scan, just to be on the safe side."

I had no problem with the scan and was relieved when Doctor Wu emailed me that the scan was negative. She suggested that I continue taking the anti-anxiety medication because stress could be the underlying cause of my headaches, and she emailed a prescription to my local pharmacy.

However, I continued to get headaches, and now I was

troubled by stomach cramps.

"Maybe the added stress of the long commute has been a factor. You never had these problems when we lived in the city," Amy was quick to remind me.

I knew where she was going, and I didn't want to have another argument about the house. I grabbed my tennis racket from the front hall closet to follow Dr. Gosh's exercise prescription.

"I'm off to play tennis with Tom. I'll see you around..."
Wham!
"#&%@!!#," I said, putting my hand to my forehead.

"Be careful," said Amy, annoyingly too late.

"I forgot to duck."

Amy just gave me the *I told you so* look again.

When the stomach cramps got to be too much, Doctor Gosh referred me to Doctor Evans, a gastroenterologist.

"I'm not sure of the underlying cause of your problem," said Doctor Evans, a balding, bespectacled fifty-something. "We'll have to run some tests on you. Here's something for stool sample collection and ask at the front desk to schedule an abdominal scan."

Doctor Evans' physician's assistant called the following week to say that the tests had come back negative, but he was recommending a proton pump inhibitor to relieve some of my stomach problems.

I can't say that the proton pump inhibitor did much for my stomach and a short time later, I had problems with constipation and heart palpitations.

When I called Doctor Evans' physician's assistant again, she recommended a laxative for the constipation and suggested I see a cardiologist.

"I see a really good cardiologist," said Ben, one of my coworkers. "He has me on statins for my heart and I've been fine since. He thinks everybody should be on statins. The only problem that I developed, though, was that Sergeant Johnson was having a hard time saluting in the bedroom, if you know what I mean. But, he prescribed that magical little blue pill, and I have to say it works great," he said, smiling too eagerly.

When I relayed this conversation to my neighbor Bill at a weekend barbecue we were hosting, he was stunned.

"How old are you?"

"Thirty-eight."

"And how many medications are you on now?"

"Four, maybe five, maybe more depending on what the cardiologist says."

"Honey, can you get some ice from the freezer inside?" yelled Amy.

"Sure," I replied, turning quickly. *Wham!* "Son of a gun!" I said holding my forehead. "I did it again."

"Wait a minute," said Bill. "How many times a week do you do that?"

"I don't know, three, maybe four or five times a week."

"I think I can not only solve your headache problem, but get you off all your other medications, too."

"No offense Bill, but you're a builder, not a doctor. They are professionals who have extensive education and training. They know what they are doing."

"Trust me. I'll be over tomorrow, and I'm pretty sure you'll be off all your medications soon."

"Okay. I'm dubious, but go for it."

Bill showed up the next day with two workers, a miter saw, 2x4s, 2x12s, crowbars, sledgehammers, nail guns, and other assorted tools.

"I want you and Amy to go out for about three hours and come back. You'll see a big difference. Trust me on this," he said.

"Okay," I replied, somewhat disbelieving.

"Oh, by the way how tall are you?"

"6'3".

Bill nodded.

Amy and I went shopping and enjoyed a pleasant lunch. When we returned, the workers were gathering up their tools and putting them away in the truck.

"So, have you performed your medical miracle?" I asked.

"Walk into your house and see if you notice the difference," Bill replied.

I walked into the house. "I don't get it," I said.

"Look at your doorways."

Each doorway had been raised up to 6'6". A new header and Sheetrock had been installed. I walked back and forth through the doorway from the living room to the kitchen several times, smiling. I no longer bumped my head.

"I put two coats of mud on the Sheetrock. I'll come back

tomorrow and put on the third. Then you sand and paint everything, and it will look great. You won't bump your head anymore and therefore, you won't have headaches. No headaches, no ibuprofen. No ibuprofen means your stomach will feel better and you won't need stomach medication. No stomach medication means no constipation or heart palpitations so you won't need a laxative or heart medication or the little blue pill."

And Bill was right.

Two weeks later, I was off all my meds and never felt better. And, we hired Bill to renovate the kitchen and bathrooms. I was pretty sure if he could pull off a medical miracle, he could pull off another miracle—making Amy fall in love with the house.

HOLY MARY, MOTHER OF GOD
John Roper

"Here, fill in another one," said Thomas as he handed me a slip of paper.

"Are we allowed to fill in more than one?" I asked.

"Definitely," he answered.

"Okay," I replied and filled in another piece of paper.

My family had just moved from Quincy, Massachusetts to Sunnyside, Long Island City, a strange new terrifying world to me. I led an idyllic life in Quincy. Our home was near a marsh where we hunted for minnows, which we used as bait when we went fishing in a nearby creek. I could walk to Red Beach and enjoy a day of swimming or walk to LaBreck Field to play baseball with my friends. I could also walk to and from Atherton Hough Elementary School every day—an action that might result in a call to the Department of Child Services today.

I now faced the mean streets of Long Island City in Queens, New York City. My parents walked with us everywhere because the city was very different. There were tough gangs that walked the streets in our neighborhood. They wore black leather jackets and carried chains and lead pipes that they didn't hesitate to use. They sang, "Love is a Many Splendored Thing" to nervous young women who crossed their paths. The smell of animal droppings and garbage assaulted our senses. Sirens, trains, and horns made sleep difficult. People were stabbed to death, their cries for help ignored. This was a scary place.

I was a stranger in a strange land looking for direction and friends. Thomas seemed to provide both, so I followed his lead by filling in the second slip of paper. I folded both pieces of paper and put them in the basket when it came around. Thomas and everyone else in the class were excited about the drawing—except me. One lucky student at Saint Theresa's of the Little Flower would be chosen to have the honor of placing a crown of flowers on the head of the Virgin Mary.

I wanted nothing to do with this. I didn't want anything to draw attention to myself. I just wanted to fit in, not to stand out or be noticed. And, I could see from the anticipation of the rest of the class that there would be disappointment, even envy or jealousy, directed at the person chosen to crown Mary.

While others were bursting with hope to be the one to crown her, the thought of walking down the aisle of the church in front of the entire student body made me anxious. What if I dropped the crown or knocked over the statue? What if the crown slipped off the pillow onto the ground? What if I tripped going up the altar and fell on my face in front of the entire student body?

Too many things could go wrong. My identity would not be John Roper, the nice, new kid from Massachusetts. It would be John Roper, the klutz from Quincy. This was too risky, and I was more than happy to have someone else do the honor.

After sister collected all the slips, she announced a special surprise. A first grader was being summoned to come to our classroom to do the drawing. There could be no hint of fixing if the winner were drawn by an innocent first grader.

The door opened and "Awww, how adorable" was uttered

by girls in my class as the first grader was walked into the room. I did not share their fascination.

"Come here," said sister. "You're going to draw the name out of this basket of the person who will crown the Virgin Mary," she explained in a sing-song rhythm.

The first-grader nodded her head that she understood.

"What is your name, sweetheart?"

"Carol."

"Carol what?"

"Carol Roper," she answered.

"Carol Roper?" asked Sister. "We have a John Roper in this class. Are you related?"

Carol scanned the room, found me, and waved. "He's my brother."

"How cute," gushed the girl next to me. *How embarrassing*, I thought.

"Well that's very nice, "said sister smiling. She placed the basket before my sister. "Put your hand in, stir up the papers, and pull out one."

My sister obeyed. She moved the slips around for several seconds, pulled out one, and handed it to Sister who unfolded it very slowly building up the tension.

"And the person to crown the Virgin Mary is… John Roper."

The class let out a gasp of surprise and disappointment.

Oh no, this can't be happening. I didn't want to do this in the first place and I can tell from the look on the faces of many of my classmates, they think the drawing was rigged. I did not want to make them angry at me.

"Sister, I don't want to do it. Please let someone else do it."

Sister looked shocked. "This is a great honor. Everyone in the school wants to crown Mary."

I struggled to find a way out. "But, I just moved here. I think the honor should go to someone who has been in the school for a longer time."

Sister shook her head. "It's true you've only been here for a short time, but you are part of the school now, and you have been chosen."

I looked at the faces around me. They looked happy when I declined and disappointed when sister answered.

"Sister, I really don't want to do it. Please choose someone else." The faces around me brightened and turned to sister. There was still hope for them.

Sister sighed and said, "All right. If that's what you wish." She then directed Carol to pick another slip.

Carol again stirred up the papers, reached in, and pulled out a slip which she handed to sister. Sister slowly unfolded the second slip. The class held its breath.

"The person who is definitely going to crown Mary tomorrow is... John Roper."

Confused, Sister looked at me. "Did you fill in two slips? she asked. "You were only supposed to fill in one."

I knew it would not help to blame Thomas. I needed friends. "I didn't know. But, I still don't want to do it."

"Oh no," sister replied. She paused as if receiving divine

inspiration. "Don't you understand? This is a sign. The Virgin Mary picked you not once, but twice." Sister smiled as if in on some secret. "She has spoken. She wants you to crown her tomorrow."

I sat down in shock trying to let everything sink in. Mary had reached out from heaven to touch someone and that someone was me. There was no way out. I would have to walk down the aisle of the church in front of everybody and crown Mary. *Oh, my God. Please don't let me screw anything up.*

I said several Hail Marys as I waited nervously the next day in the back of the church for the signal to come to the altar. Finally, father waved me forward and I walked to the altar carrying Mary's crown of flowers on a satin pillow.

All eyes were on me. Every step seemed to take forever as I concentrated as hard as I could at the task at hand. *Take precise steps, keep the pillow steady, look where you're going, breathe.*

I made it to the altar without tripping or falling. The crown did not slip off the pillow, and when I placed it on Mary's head, I could've sworn that she smiled at me.

Everything went well and my classmates didn't seem to resent me. In fact, I seemed to fit in and make new friends fairly quickly. And, I now realized how badly I needed a new ally.

Saint Theresa's was an old school heavy with darkness and gloom even in 1955. It felt like a prison and was run like one. We were made to sit in silence unless spoken to. We lined up to go to the cafeteria where we sat in silence as we ate. We lined up to go to the restroom in silence and lined up to turn to the classroom.

Somehow, Christ's message of love was transformed into a reign of terror in this school. We were slapped across the face or whacked on the hands with rulers if we forgot to do our homework, did it incorrectly, or for any arbitrary infraction made up on the spot by any nun who didn't like something we had just done.

I lived in constant fear. I would do my homework as soon as I came home. I would check it and double check it after dinner, then check it again before bed. I would often wake at night, afraid I had forgotten something and riffle through my assignment pad and binder to make sure I had done everything. I would check again before I left for school and then again when I got to school.

I realized I now had a way out. Mary, the mother of God, would help me. Every morning and night, I said innumerable Hail Marys to achieve one dream: to move to California, become a Mouseketeer, and make Annette Funicello my girlfriend. I watched the *Mickey Mouse Club* at 5 o'clock every day. For sixty magic minutes, I was transported from the prison of Saint Theresa's and the difficulties of Long Island City to the wondrous world of Disney. I prayed with the religious intensity known only to saints and martyrs that my dream would come true.

One day, my father came home and announced we were moving.

Thank you, Mary, thank you, thank you, thank you. My prayers had been answered!

However, we were not moving to California but to Dobbs Ferry, New York. Annette would have to wait.

Dobbs Ferry was not California, but there were no gangs, sirens, traffic jams, or stabbings...and the nuns were nice. I went to Saint Matthew's in Hastings on the Hudson. The classroom was new, bright, and sunny. The nuns did not hit us, and I made friends right away. I enjoyed the school and didn't fear getting hit.

Sometimes I wonder why Mary sent us to Dobbs Ferry and not California. Was it because I rejected Mary the first time? Was Mary inundated with requests from millions who also wanted to be Mouseketeers? Did half the boys in America have a crush on Annette? Was Mary aware that I had never taken a dance, voice, or acting lesson, and she spared me the disappointment of crushing rejection? Did she save me the embarrassment of co-starring with Annette in *Beach Blanket Bingo*?

Maybe Dobbs Ferry wasn't so bad after all.

"It's surprising how much memory is built around things unnoticed at the time."
— **Barbara Kingsolver**

Myrna Brown and her husband, Denis, moved to Wilmington in 2010. She retired from an active life as a nurse manager in hospice care. Prior to her career as a nurse, Myrna was the managing editor of a local newspaper in Scotts Valley, California. She then became a writer/editor for the United States Air Force at the Onizuka Satellite Control Facility in Sunnyvale, California. She was assigned to a position at the Pentagon in Virginia to write, together with a team of five, the Air Force Report to Congress as well as briefing papers for USAF officers giving testimony to Congress.

At age 70, she began to write fiction. She has just self-published a novel, *Side Effects,* her third novel in three years. She is currently vice president of programs for the Coastal Carolina Women's Club. When she has time, she volunteers at the Wilmington Assistance League in their thrift shop. She belongs to Great Oaks Women's Club, the local branch of Association of American University Women. She also served on the national board of AAUW Educational Foundation for three years.

Myrna and her husband support Medicine for Mali, a project that works to provide prenatal, delivery, and postnatal care to women who have no access to medical care.

THE FERRIS WHEEL
Myrna Brown

The service was in the confines of a narrow, nearly dark chapel. Those attending were slowly filing by, row by row, one by one, to glimpse her body. The powdered rouge was applied too high on her cheeks, the satin pillow a little too cushiony. The feet were blanketed where her sassy sandals might have been.

The light couldn't penetrate. The windows were but slits, and an inlaid disc of stained glass, dim and flat in color, was testimony that the sky was overcast and gray as if it were dusk. The altar made no shadow, nor could you see the emblem of the cross scored into the wood. There *were* no marked shadows; if you looked up, even the timbers that formed the structure were obscure. Pale lights hung from the beams, their halos unworldly as if crowded by living dust.

She was dressed in linen, beige and white. At first the only color in the room seemed to be those flaming cheeks. However, half hidden under buttoned coats, the colors of the ties of the men hinted at an early winter. In artful taste, the silk streaked their chests, framed by well-designed suits the color of coal. Otherwise, there was only the somber paleness of the indoors.

The sweet smell of wood from the curved rafters lay just beneath that of the presumptuous smell of roses. Someone had remembered she loved gardenias. They were handpicked and put in a small crystal vase placed very near the head of the casket. If one leaned in slightly, as did her lover, Jim, it seemed the fragile petals perfumed her hair. Her hair was still lustrous and beautifully done, but not in the casual way she would have styled it. Otherwise, too, it would have smelled like ocean air, the freshness of which no one can describe.

Jim was in line. They had recently broken apart. As grief swept in, he remembered their lovemaking, recalled taking pleasure touching the velvet skin and smelling the jasmine in her perfume. Inconsolable, but not outwardly overcome, he ran his left hand along the brass rail of the casket as he passed. He saw the glint of gold of his wedding ring, never removed for over thirty-five years. He felt the old conflict, confused momentarily, but resolute to keep his composure. Boring down, the profundity of his loss made him slightly nauseous. It was if he had emptied his gut.

Unbeknownst to the living, the ghost of her deceased husband, Steve, was among other ghosts that inhabited the shadows. The ghosts of her parents and those of friends commingled near the rafters as they waited for her body to be taken from the chapel. When would her spirit ascend?

Rubbing auras with other ghosts was no one's cup of tea. Spirits are often coarse; jaded in the afterlife after having expected more power and influence while on earth. Now everyone was of the same class. Steve's ghost jostled for a place low in the front.

"Excuse you," the deceased's mother's spirit said.

Steve's ghost bumped his way forward. He believed he had had first place in her heart. Jim was, and had been, unaware she had held her first husband in something of a perpetual spiritual suspension. She had used her memories of Steve as a measure for any other companion.

Jim, the lover who had recently been shut out, was blind to her propensity to dawdle in her mind over her deceased husband. Steve had satisfied her every need. The memories of Steve stayed locked down in the most mundane of tasks. He remained the principal person in her affections.

Jim had believed they were of one spirit. Now, his heart felt hacked in half. She was gone. Little did he know there was such a ghost as Steve's, let alone a resentful ghost. He hadn't known Steve's ghost had been his competition.

Steve's ghost had been given to tagging after the amorous couple, sometimes disruptive, especially distracting Jim in the height of the moment when he felt most his prowess. Maybe the phone would ring. He couldn't arrange everything. Her foot would itch as if a feather had passed across it.

Once, after Jim had gone, she found a feather near the foot of the bed and wondered aloud. Maybe it was on Jim's shoe. But no, it had blown in the open window. Steve could blow. It was one of his powers.

Having failed after the small disruptions in their lovemaking, she would stroke the limpness of the forlorn Jim, saying, "Don't worry. We always have tomorrow."

"Yes, but I'll be around." Steve's ghost would say just below the Chopin that played through the speakers over the bed, resetting the phone in its cradle.

The service was over, and the organist became more dramatic in the conclusion of "A Mighty Fortress is Our God," holding down a final chord of dark notes. Jim felt the solemnity in the quietness, not realizing the heaviness of the silence was added upon by the ghosts milling about.

The long black Cadillac would come to take the sealed box, and those still living would be released momentarily from the tension of holding back their private grief. They trailed outdoors after passing by her body, the men holding their hands in front of their trousers, one laid over the other, looking like ushers, respectful. Others who attended appeared reluctant to enter the aisle, motioning those in the row in front of them to go first.

As they gathered outside, waiting in the shade, Jim's petite wife, Laura, moved near his elbow, which he had forgotten to extend. Everything she wore matched down to the sensible Salvador Feragamos. Her interest was piqued in the moment after seeing her mate linger a bit over the body and touching the brass edge of the coffin. Had he leaned slightly forward or had she conjured it?

Laura was envious of the dead woman even though the deceased, a middle-aged widow, had not knowingly been a challenge to her well-being. Laura was a good mother who had nurtured and shepherded her family through infancy to university. She believed herself to be deservedly fortified by how well she had loved her own and made a home. She moved to join the other women. There were no children in attendance to punctuate the silence, no rustling or fidgeting.

Of a certain age, Caucasian, and well-mannered, Laura had her coffers full. She had come into her middle years, secure and hopeful. In restaurants, Jim stood if she got up to use the facilities. In church, he opened the hymnal and they sang together. If they attended a gala, they danced well together. Jim was dependably respectable. He was head deacon.

Laura's friends, others' wives in her set, had worked together with the deceased as volunteers in various jobs, chairing the annual bazaar, wheeling patients released from the hospital to a waiting car, taking knitted shawls to the elderly women among the congregation should they fall ill. They didn't realize they were on the threshold of being old. They couldn't imagine themselves in nursing homes or being cared for by strangers.

They just couldn't identify with a sedentary life in a large chair left to shiver all day, all the while on the brink of breaking a hip or stroking. No, Laura's cohort felt secure. They hadn't had many losses. Having lost their parents seemed the natural way of things. Life didn't seem to have a precipice.

They had only known the deceased in a superficial way. Outside the chapel, Laura and the other women remained curious and quiet, vigilant. *What was in the air?* When the time came for the hearse to pull away, they sorted themselves out and each took the arm of their respective husband.

Jim was standing apart with a cigar. He lit it, drew in deeply before exhaling, and held the smoke in his chest as if he were reflecting. When he blew the smoke, it surrounded him like mist. Stephen's ghost had blown the smoke back into his face. Jim squinted, flagged the air and pulled again on the cigar. Jim had been with her as often as he could for over a year. Only a month had passed when he had looked into his empty glass and retreated, knowing full well she was showing him the door. He had laid his key on the antique credenza. If he had turned, which he didn't, she would have seen his tears.

Following the procession to the waiting hearse, it was as if Steve's ghost, though invisible, were panting as he lusted after his bygone senses. Perhaps the wind had picked up, the living thought, when they felt the chill. The small host of spirits was obsessed by its need to intrude into what belongs only to the earth: a ceremony of death. Even so, they descended and haunted the space around the coffin, as if she were ready to be raised up. When would her spirit lift to join them? They flitted above her as the flowers were being carted out by the black-suited men of the funeral home.

It was all so formal. An ash from Jim's cigar dropped onto his black and gold tie, a gift from her. He brushed it, and it left a stain. He threw down the cigar and left it as litter.

The gravesite was but a short distance away. The ghosts would be there, too. The air stirred as they made their way ahead of the hearse. Steve's ghost led the way. Perhaps it was the ghosts' presence that caused everyone to only whisper or stand silently. The Presbyterian minister stood before the hole, which seemed to beg to be filled.

During the last year, Jim had been channeled into her stream, as it were, passing through her soul like moving water. In her company, he had experienced himself according to nature's way, being dumped into a sea of ecstasy followed by sublimity.

Jim was on the cusp of retirement, his body beginning to show wear. He had drunk her in, so thirsty he had been for what she offered. He had taken deep draughts of hope on his walks, cavorted in her bed, dressed her inspired concoction of a salad in the kitchen and sat with a crystal glass in hand on her porch. Speaking of drinks, she was like the warmth of a Manhattan, soothing from the first sip, amber-like in color, transparent but mysterious. Being with her was a bit like being transformed, softly inebriating.

The time came when they both knew the exclusivity of their world would become like a wadi in the desert, doomed to dry up. There are seasons in one's life, and the dry season had come back around. Jim had been sent away after telling her he could no longer abide the contradictions within himself. She couldn't abide him being torn, even though she was trapped in her own circular thoughts about Steve. Even the turn of the key sparked hope it was Steve returning to her.

Steve drifted around the grave site. He craved to cradle against her narrow back, craved the emotions of being enthralled by her; he craved to re-experience an epiphany, for love can seem to be a sudden reaffirmation, as if God has visited and everything becomes clear. But the anguish of a ghost is his damning memory and wishful thinking about the past. Forever impotent, vaguely remembered, a ghost rides forever in a chariot of fire, never arriving.

The desire to connect was stronger than in life. Floating in air, Steve's ghost had been present, secretly present, when Jim was around, aching to partake of life again. He wanted for the hushed moments he'd had with her that most represented the coming together of his soul with his body.

For Jim, being with her had been like being in an only-imagined perfect afterworld and at the same time being physically present: heaven and earth at the same time. Her presence had been all things in one fell swoop.

Because Steve's ghost was so persistent, she would sigh as

she remembered them coupled even as she coupled with Jim. Or, she might have been in her car going across the bridge, sad and torn, when his most precious of faces would appear beside her. He would have reached to put a hand on her thigh. She would have taken a hand off the wheel and stroked his sideburn with one finger. He might have put the finger in his mouth, laying his head back.

Though it pained him, Steve's ghost experienced her vicariously as often as possible. No wonder it was hard for her to forget him. He forever inserted himself into her private life, haunting without inducing fear, watching her read a book, stretching in the morning. Sometimes he straightened her closet and lined up her shoes. He might turn on the hose and water her hydrangeas.

She would be made to remember them together, taking their coffee still in their robes or Steve getting ready to go to his office, tying his tie in the full length mirror as she stood in her slip behind him, watching while he twisted his neck as men do, straightening the knot, smoothing the band of silk down with the flat of a hand.

His invisible invasions left him feeling ashamed. Damn, he still had his conscience. What would it be like to go about without a conscience? Death hadn't freed him. It was unsatisfactory for him to glide forever in a realm where only his talent for prompting memories was manifest, that and move the air or send charges of electricity. She might be surprised when a light bulb winked on and off or the dish washer came on. He could move the air, stir up the dust. He couldn't make Jim go away.

As most ghosts, Steve took pride in the particular power to persuade and alter thoughts. As a ghost he could evoke the smell of a guava in the tropics or of roasting pork in a mountainside restaurant overlooking a valley in Germany. He could rock the senses, tricking the eye to catch a glimpse of a reminder of him and the like. He might be in a favorite local café, waiting for her. She was the only one he hovered over. But the provocation of thoughts about him was just one of his skills. With clarity, pitch on, he brought back the utterances of himself, the dear lost one, and tripped her tongue as emotion overcame her. She was never able to tell Jim she loved him. It wouldn't gush out.

As a matter of fact, while ghosts are inside the minds of those still trekking through life, they re-sculpt the memories attached to their shrines designed by the living. In similar fashion, Steve's ghost shaped and tooled a new version of himself until she thought of him as an ideal. Ghosts do tamper most often with the memories of those held by old friends and family. By persuasive but unknowable influence, they enhance the scenes where they are portrayed from memory, developing themes, adding irony and humor, even depth of character. Their lies increase their aura. The memories recounted by the affected are more flattering. Steve's ghost was no exception. He had an array of tactics. He manipulated her thoughts, even as she squeezed a lime for a gin and tonic.

As is the practice of many ghosts, he put himself in only the best light. Ghosts usually entice people to reconstruct their images. Hazily, those loved ones left behind stretch to the back of their minds to play a memory. In accord with the voice of the ghost; a newly introduced fresh notion alters that memory favorably forever. *He was always generous* they might say. *He was a gentleman.* People didn't remember how he deducted the tax before he tipped. He didn't chisel people out of their money, but he was tight and saved his best wines for himself. Over time, those memories were erased or permanently altered.

Finally, through their meddling, the dead stand more proudly in the minds of others, especially kinfolk. Time gives the reconstructed memories even more credence, and they fit themselves into the crevices of those livings' brains and make them laugh out loud or crouch and shield their faces to cry in sorrow. Ghosts like inducing strong emotions, a sob or a husky voice. Leave them alone with someone and ghosts will ride a memory to death.

As for Jim, he had delved more deeply than before into his soul with her as inspiration and guide. She had chosen him. He felt chosen, anyway. That first time they locked eyes as she worked in the church kitchen he had been changed, he believed, and came through his time with her less estranged from himself, affected deeply and permanently.

At the height of Jim's career but at the lowest ebb of the challenges, she came into his sight. Just when he'd set the world right, had money in the bank, his children educated, his wife contentedly busy with other women doing their part for society's sake. She had seemed to be the something that was missing. Elated, he felt privileged to learn from and know her. The possibility of supreme pleasure in that chapter of life was a revelation, stirring him profoundly. He was renewed. They sired dreams as offspring. The dreams were born into the light on an excursion to the seaside or alongside a pure stream. *How could life be so sweet, the pleasure rendered so effortlessly?*

And it was in her arms, the familiar sense of being deprived of real love lifted. He was just discovering he hadn't ever lived life to the full. In the silence of peace and satisfaction there is reverence, and in the space of his time with her, he worshipped her.

She had smoothed her hand down his paunch and before several weeks went by, it was neither so large nor as tight. Jim had thought to himself, *if this isn't real, then what is? Becoming fit, being in love, I'll live forever.*

She required his energy. He lusted after his younger self, even to the point he imagined being on the basketball court, shooting a three pointer. Inevitably being her lover entailed the taking of time, time he stole, providing in a new way the compensation only passionate love can bring. The experience was a bonus that the gift of a Rolex or a new car could not compare.

More to life than signing contracts, overseeing the construction of an apartment complex, he rationalized his choice, inspired, newly ambitious.

He came into his old vigor with a touching sensitivity he had not known he was capable of. Nor had he known the intricate ways of lovemaking. He learned to take his time. He became deliberate. He went home to his wife, and his touch was more delicate and seductive. He had paused to look back on his life; the heretofore unidentified desire had been there like a hole he hadn't filled.

The pilings had shifted as Jim aged, but he got his footing

again when with her. He yearned constantly for her, at his desk, listening to Beethoven in the car, taking out the garbage, walking Duchess, their German shepherd.

He was a kind, gentle man, in wonderment he hadn't explored or been wooed before by such an attraction as she. Everything became new. Life strutted out before him with a wink and a nod. He can't be blamed for following. Life is short. It was a flash flood of lust, yes, but more. It was the sweetness of the rain on the dry soul of his spirit. It was the morning sun on a sunflower.

Eventually, Jim had paid the ungodly price of detaching from her and reconciling himself to a mundane destiny. His fantasies now lay dormant in his groin. But he revered life more and nurtured his body respectfully. He was more attentive to his wife. The gift the other woman had given was not retractable.

After saying goodbye, he had rectified his doings; he had come back into alignment with what is the norm for men of a certain stature. He hadn't paid the higher price of claiming her in public. No, his life as he knew it would have gone away. In the chapel, secretly, stalled briefly before her body, he wished he had abandoned all for her love. Alas, he was not that brave. The exposed alliance would have been his undoing.

After the onset of his struggle with his conscience, she released him easily like fish on a line, gently returning him to the larger realm of the sea. She understood she was a healer, someone who rejuvenated. Though he didn't know, her investment had been temporary. She was not one who could ever love again as she had her first love. She was the silent pause between movements in a concert hall, not the conclusive horns and drums.

Go back, she wrote in neat little script, French-like, on the tablet at the bedside. *Take this truth with you, that life is lived but once. Acknowledge all of yourself, not just the aspect your colleagues see, or the person your children and your wife encounter. You have had this experience with me that authenticated your ability to love totally. You abandoned yourself here and look how you slept in my bed, at peace.*

As it happened, you wakened to the sizzle in the fry pan; you came to my elbow and flipped the cutlet over; you squeezed the lemon; you snipped the parsley; we dined at the wrought iron table in the sunroom. As the sunset fell across your face, I knew to release you. Importantly, your capacity to be loved was proved to you. We finished the wine. You tipped your goblet toward you only to see it was gone. And so I write, the glass is empty. Goodbye and be happy.

At the grave site where the smell of freshly turned soil made one nostalgic, before the hearse pulled up, the ghost of her first husband, Steve, encroached on the scene, remembering time after time, when he felt that death on earth was held at bay when with her. He flushed a bee from its flower and it buzzed over Jim's bald head. He had it in for him. The roses and lilies trembled and petals floated and fell into the loosened dirt. The birds in the leafless tree nearby left in a rush. The red cardinal returned as if to witness the lowering of the coffin.

What had happened to Steve? Steve's twin engine plane had failed him. He had skidded atop the river, swept west in its current toward the sea, knowing he would be unconscious when he drowned. Tragic, everyone said, compelled to care about her well-being after such loss.

Jim may have believed he had an intention to comfort her. But in truth, his first instincts were sexual in nature. He remembered Steve and she had looked handsome together at the various cocktail parties and church functions.

After a time, his tragic death behind her, she began coming to the church suppers alone. She was bent over the oven in the church kitchen when he noticed her pushing her hair back. The surge of desire was a surprise to him.

She seemed to know the heart of a man. Her art was to bring him into a fullness he'd not thought possible. For her, she simply replaced his face with former images of her deceased husband. Remembering her rapture with Steve, she introduced all her intimate measures to Jim. No one thinks to teach someone about the ways of love, but she did, and as she lay with Jim, Steve's presence seemed to come back, briefly like a whisper. She welcomed the spirit of him, even smiled at his small manipulations and mischievous ways.

She knew her future would be as a single woman, and she had taken her time to heal after Steve's death. She traveled alone, adjusting to being single, cruising from Barcelona to Amsterdam, the strangers on board never coming to know her status as a widow. She had plunged into the excursions, going to the Reich museum, climbing into the attic of Anne Frank's home. She lost her balance as she stood near the nave in Gaudi's cathedral. A stranger supported her.

She knew she had led Jim to experience the existential bliss of his outer man fusing with his inner man, to be changed thereafter, newly challenged in a more humble manner than before she cared for him. She loved by intention but did not lose herself to Jim; not ever again would she love as she had.

Jim's conscience only allowed him to love Laura. Never before this second venture into loving a woman had he adored someone. Jim had cried as he lay on her breasts, but her empathy never stretched to love. The statue in her mind dedicated to her memories of her first love never crumbled. His whispers could be evoked in the rustle of leaves, in the scatting of a rabbit across her drive, the brush of a branch against her window. But it was crossing the river that took her breath away.

As it happened, several days prior to the occasion of her funeral, her black Mercedes crashed against the concrete divider just as she was beginning to cross the bridge. She had looked away from the road, distracted by the gray river where they'd not found Steve.

Yes, she said, that's where you died, right out there in the cold Columbia River. To her, the water coiled like a snake around the uninhabited islands. The sky was puffy, bursting with sunlight that skimmed the surface of the great river, adding a layer of sheen like a cloth across an altar. Then it was as if someone had taken the wheel. She saw the abutment and gave in to the inevitable.

The seatbelt held her steady and firm against the leather bucket seat. Her first love presented full face. The motor was pushed forward, crushing her legs.

Steve was the one who hadn't chosen to leave her. She had learned all she conveyed to Jim about tenderness from Steve. She had only ever loved Steve. Just how had the steering wheel turned so quickly in her hand?

Thus came about the service in the little chapel which held the man, Jim, who had so loved her. The ceremony had rendered the incipient opportunity for Steve's ghost to charge the air. He had waited and watched long enough.

We don't know if she was assigned to the same realm as Steve, but surely she was. I would imagine they leave Jim and Laura's nest undisturbed and just enjoy life in the clouds dangling their legs in what must seem like a giant Ferris wheel.

IN THE DISQUIET OF MY MIND
Myrna Brown

In the disquiet of my mind, I have lost the rhythm of my inner voice. Thoughts are like the touch-and-goes of a butterfly on my fingertip, whose embroidered wings arc up and away. I follow with my eyes to see on which bloom it feeds.

Similarly to that golden sun-drenched creature that goes from flower to flower, I fool my halting thoughts into believing that I am not dusky and colorless and that I can smell the saccharine in the air. I flit toward near-turned aging blossoms, which will not have the sweetness I desire.

I know I am entrapped in this winter garden still saturated in autumn colors, but let me pretend to return to a different season to feed on what were my stations of red hibiscus, hollyhocks, lilies and gladiolas. I must if I am to survive.

Let me still my thoughts as if to hover, as was my habit, to feed of summer's nectar. Give me back yesterday's familiar draughts of nature; let me feed nonchalantly guided by the scents I knew. Let me taste again with more leisure. A rose would be my bed.

Let me return to what was my own pulsing garden, to the sureness of my intuitions, the beat of my own wings. Let light rays be bent again to permeate my transparency and restore my color. Let my dreams survive. Let my thoughts be anticipatory.

If not, let me accept the most obvious of metaphors in nature. Stop my off-beat, unrhymed resistance to its course. Someone goes before and someone comes behind, for that is nature's most grand illustration to us. The beginning of the end is its most definite season.

"Now this is not the end. It is not even the beginning of the end. But it is, perhaps, the end of the beginning."
— **Winston Churchill**

Did you enjoy *Reflections of Life*?

Send us an email to let us know!
LandfallWriters@gmail.com

Also, be sure to order our first book, *Pieces of Life*
Available at **www.blurb.com**